Achieving EXCELLENCE *in Life*

MARK MAXON

Your Guide • 12 Sessions • Infinite Possibilities!

Published in cooperation with
Lifeworks International, Inc.

www.themaxongroup.com

© 2008 Mark A. Maxon

Achieving Excellence in Life

Your Personal Coach—

Achieving Excellence in Life—

Dedication

To my beautiful wife Tresha and our children.

I love you.

CONTENTS

A LETTER TO YOU

For several years I have wanted to share the knowledge I have come to recognize as critical for living a life abundant with love and prosperity. I have stated countless times that I would get around to it when the timing was right. The timing is never right unless we choose to make it so. As you can see, I have made my choice.

You too have made your choice — to pick up this book and examine its contents. I hope you will invest the time to use this book as it has been designed to be used. This is not the type of book you will want to read and set aside; it was created as a guide for those who aspire to live in excellence. To accomplish this, you will be asked to participate in the final drafting of what I have only begun. The end result will be the writing of your autobiography — your life as you would make it.

Should you choose to follow my instructions, inspired by principles that have been handed down to you and me by many of the greatest individuals to grace human history, you will never be the same. So ask yourself, are you currently living the life you have dreamed of? Should you resemble the majority of individuals I have met, you are seeking something more from life. Perhaps it is love, purpose, freedom, self-expression, or money you are searching for. Whatever it may be, within these pages you will be introduced to principles that will permit you to live the life you have previously only dreamt of living.

ACKNOWLEDGEMENTS

I would like to extend my gratitude to many people. The few I mention does not reflect the true number of exceptional individuals who have played a role in shaping the person I am today. To those of you I have not named, I extend my appreciation for the friendship you have shown me, and I thank you for understanding it is simply not feasible to acknowledge each of you by name.

To my beautiful wife, Tresha—thank you for being my closest confidante and best friend. We have shared many good times and some tough times; still, I cannot think of a bad day since I met you. You and our children have brought me joy, purpose, and ultimately, a passion for life I had not known before. I express my love to all of you and to the source responsible for our introduction.

Thank you to my daughter Destiny, my friends Janette, John and Robert; each of you encouraged me to reach for the stars. I also extend a special thank-you to all of the positive people who are striving to make a difference in this world.

Last but by no means least; I salute each of you who have committed to reading this book. May all that is good be yours.

INTRODUCTION

All people would love to live their dreams. Unfortunately, too many people will never accomplish the things they at one time aspired to achieve. The masses complain it is because they do not posses the necessary knowledge or that they have not had the right break; yet in reality it is because they fail to put forth the effort. Knowledge is accessible to those who choose to seek it.

I have written this book for many reasons. First, I wish to provide you with the motivation and inspiration necessary to create the life you have always desired. Second, I wish to equip you with the tools necessary for achieving feats you once felt you were incapable of accomplishing. Ultimately, the choice will be yours as to whether you act upon the instruction offered herein. For those of you who do, you can look forward to becoming increasingly proficient at creating your own opportunities. As a result you will find yourself living in greater abundance.

This book is a culmination of my personal and professional experience. The principles and methods include the teachings of many of the most remarkable figures throughout human history, as well as my personal insights gained through the application of these principles and methods.

Your Personal Coach: Achieving Excellence in Life – Twelve Sessions, Infinite Possibilities is designed to coach you—with your permission, of course—in multiple areas, personally and professionally. This book will assist you in achieving heightened levels of performance and lead to unprecedented success in your life!

Have you ever wondered what your life would look like were you to achieve your true potential? If so, this book is for you. Business owners, executives, sales professionals, athletes, students, homemakers, and everyone anywhere, this book is for you! Every day individuals around the world retain the services of consultants and coaches to improve their performance—and for good reason. Though obtaining a qualified personal coach may appear financially unrealistic for many, the resulting benefits frequently outweigh the initial investment. I have witnessed the substantial return such an investment can generate financially, physically, and emotionally. The resulting benefits certainly cannot be measured in the monetary gain alone.

Interestingly enough, the change experienced in thought is what provides the financial prosperity many seek. When you believe or think you cannot afford and or accomplish something, you are likely to assure this continues to remain your reality. Thought determines our action or lack thereof, and actions yield results. Consequently, if you do not care for the results you are getting, look first to your thoughts.

This book is your opportunity to have your own personal coach advising you daily for the next twelve weeks and beyond. The only investment you will make, from this point forward, will be to complete the exercises at the end of each section. To maximize your results you will want to adhere to the structure as it is presented. Follow my recommendations; they have worked for me and for the countless individuals I have coached for the better part of a decade.

Now, thirty years into my career (the past ten years as a personal coach, sales trainer, and business consultant), I have witnessed just about every excuse imaginable for individuals failing to achieve their dreams. I wrote this book for the person who aspires to achieve something significant with their life — for the individual who chooses, as the saying goes, to become larger than life. I reveal principles that consistently provide the positive results you desire and thus consequently permit you to live your dreams.

I have read hundreds of self-improvement and business-development books, and over the course of my career I have attended countless personal-development seminars. Years of experience in life and business have afforded me the opportunity to build relationships resulting in thousands of transactions, consisting of both tangible products and intangible services. There are dramatic parallels in leading a successful life and operating a successful business. Both can be reduced to fundamental simplicities promoting success. Life and business at their best take on a natural flow. When we witness success in either, it commands our attention, as it should. The principles that provide a workable foundation for a successful business additionally provide for excellence in life. Many people fail to implement the principles in both.

There is a formula for success that eludes most people — primarily because they fail to recognize the simplicity of the physical laws comprising it. Throughout recorded history, many have understood and implemented this formula. As a result, they have obtained riches beyond the comprehension of the majority. This formula awaits your desire and active embrace. The formula does exist, it does work, and it cannot deny you what you seek, for the formula cannot violate the physical laws which govern it. You simply must understand how to co-operate with the laws themselves, and abundance will be yours! Sound simple? Well, the process is far less complex than the majority would lead us to believe.

There is a sequential pattern to the formula. Composed of thought and action, it draws one's dreams into reality. I will not challenge the perception that success can be haphazardly obtained; however, random success is unlikely to last. You will find it difficult, if not impossible, to duplicate positive results with any consistency when operating by the seat of your pants. Doing so is comparable to flying a plane without instrumentation in a storm; you may make for your destination, but you probably will not reach it. The formula, or system, contained within these pages provides you the ability to achieve your dreams with precision. This formula works within the framework of natural law and is as real as the gravity that permits our existence on planet Earth.

You undoubtedly know someone who utilizes the formula in life and business. Such people always seem to get most, if not all, of what they demand from life. Great opportunities are frequently, perhaps consistently, presented to these individuals. They always live in abundance, surrounded with the tangible accoutrements of wealth and in the company of loving companions. Often the subject of envy, they are labeled the "lucky" ones. "It must be luck or simply good fortune," we may think to ourselves or say to another. We may ask them how they do it! To which they may reply, "I don't know, it just seems to come together for me. I guess I'm just lucky."

It is more than luck, I assure you. I am not saying they have been dishonest in their reply; it is possible they have emulated the behavior of another without having understood its relevance. I have witnessed those who are in alignment with the critical elements of the formula and yet are not consciously aware of the role the elements play in the attainment of their desires.

I presume you acquired this book in order to learn how to get more of what you demand out of life. Perhaps a friend, relative, or business associate presented you with this copy. Regardless of how you came to possess it, the message contained within found its way to you for a reason. There is something you desire. Perhaps you are seeking love, health, money, recognition, or freedom. Something is missing in your life. You may not be sure what it is; you just feel empty. Whatever your situation, you will find the answers you seek within the pages of this book; it contains many insights. Most importantly, this book contains the right questions, quality questions posed to your conscious and unconscious mind that encourage a constructive response. Solutions currently lying dormant within you will awaken.

You are about to embark on a remarkable journey. You will enter into a new state of self-awareness, experience a personal awakening to the true purpose of your life, and learn how to live in accordance with the laws governing success. You will become intimately familiar with what I call "Life's Critical Elements," which have truly changed the lives of those who have chosen to embrace them. You will learn how to combine specific principles, which when aligned, create unprecedented power: power to love, power to create, and power to live unconfined by perceptions which suppress the spirit and bind the soul.

Lessons in life taught me education may be derived from many tributaries and is not restricted to a formal process. Many people achieve higher standards of performance within the framework of a structured curriculum, while many others do quite well in an informal experiential environment. Regardless of your educational background, to become a champion and maintain your performance as a champion, you must have quality coaching. Welcome to your new life of abundance and prosperity. Congratulations on choosing *Your Personal Coach: Achieving Excellence in Life.*

GREATNESS RISES FROM ADVERSITY

Like many people, my childhood presented what easily could have been insurmountable obstacles. I faced circumstances which, I have been told, should have left me emotionally scared. My early life provided me with an ample foundation and an accompanying excuse for self-destructive behavior. To provide you with insight into who I am and what inspired me to write this book, I will share some details of my early life.

I have experienced both poverty and prosperity. Born in California in 1960 to a middle-class family, I was my mother's fifth child and the only of her relationship with my father. My father died tragically when I was just three, and my mother remarried shortly thereafter. She did not manage well without a man in her life, or for that matter, with a man either.

I was bounced around from relative to relative, a month or two here, six months there. Fortunately, there were people who cared about me; yet it was not easy for them to come to my aid because my mother would disrupt their lives, as she did mine, with bouts of depression and anger. Nevertheless, I truly love my mother. What happened is passed and forgiven; yet it is relevant to what we will be discussing.

My mother's first husband and the father of her first four children, was and is today, a good man. Based on my siblings' accounts, as well as my own personal experiences with him, I have no reason to believe otherwise. My mother, on the other hand, would describe him in a less-flattering light. I imagine there is truth in both accounts.

I have compassion for the detrimental impact their divorce had on the lives of my brothers and sisters. I understand the anger they must have felt for my father and the role he played. You see, I am the son of the man who my siblings believe deprived them of their mother. Though it pains me that they suffered, I cannot wish their pain away anymore than I can my own. Furthermore, this experience has played a significant role in shaping the person I have become.

I share an abbreviated autobiography so you may have a greater understanding of the obstacles I have faced. I am not seeking your sympathy. I only hope you will draw some parallel to your own life, which will permit you to embrace the message awaiting you within these pages. I know there are countless people who have suffered far more than you or I can comprehend. Still, I am convinced each of us, if we choose, can become better for having experienced adversity. Those who continue to strive for deliverance from the despair, depression, isolation, and self-destructive behavior characteristic of adversity, read on. You will find your salvation in the chapters to come.

From my mother, I learned she and my father met as patients in a psychiatric hospital while still married to her first husband. Upon her discharge, my mother relocated to California to be near my father. I was born out of wedlock in the spring of 1960—an embarrassment to both sides of the family. My father, the son of a well-to-do real estate broker, was, as my mother would describe him, a handsome, deep-thinking man who had built and operated his own business. She would tell me stories in later years of his great physical strength, intelligence, and humor. Unfortunately, this is not all she would describe. I would also hear of his temper, intolerance, philandering, depression, and alcoholism—just as I would later witness and hear from others of my mother's own emotional exploits and psychological instability.

When I was three years old, my father took his life while I was home in his care. I did not witness the actual act, but vividly recall being locked out of the garage, unable to find him. I remember standing and circling in the driveway while crying and calling for him when a neighbor found me. I am sure it was not difficult to assess the severity of the situation—the sound of a running car engine and the odor of exhaust fumes escaping from a closed garage—would lead to the logical conclusion that something was amiss. For years the image of the fire engines remained vividly imprinted in my memory. I was not permitted to attend my father's funeral, and it was many years before I would visit his gravesite.

My mother remarried shortly after my father's death. She married a man she met at her place of employment while living with my father. My mother was a cocktail waitress; my stepfather, the club manager. I must admit he was a charming sort — good looking, charismatic, and intelligent. From Mexico City, he spoke with a thick accent characteristic of a leading man in a motion picture. His charm was appealing and at times comforting. He was quite good to me but not to my mother. For four years she would run from him and then return. I can remember the terror I experienced countless times seeing her beaten before my eyes, often to the point of being almost unrecognizable.

I do not believe there was ever a physical injury, among the many she endured, that could have matched the damage done to her spirit. Mother could match the vulgarity of the vilest men at the corner bar after a drinking binge on a Saturday night. I have heard such language only a few times in my life. Though both she and my stepfather shared responsibility for their marital conflict, she should have left for good long before she did.

I feel for my mother's parents. They endured great torment at the plight of their daughter, and all the while they wanted desperately to help. But they could not help her; she had to help herself. We must all help ourselves.

Between my mother's escapades, she might find time for me. Too often I would be subject to the projection of her insecurities. Many times throughout my childhood she would compare me to my father, often pointing out the weaknesses rather than the strengths we had in common. When I struggled with school, she told me I was stupid; where I excelled socially, she accused me of insincerity. I was damned either way. I have long since come to understand her harshness was the result of fear. Afraid of life, afraid for herself, and afraid for me, my mother was emotionally crippled. She would periodically get herself together just long enough to express she was proud of me and loved me, and to this day I do not question her love for me.

Despite our tremulous lives, we were fortunate to live in some interesting places in California: Santa Monica, Hollywood, Laguna Hills, Malibu, and for a time with my father's sister, her husband, and my cousins in Beverly Hills. I attended a public elementary school in Beverly Hills.

My uncle's father owned the house we lived in. We referred to it as "The Big House," and that is exactly what it was. Purchased by Marian Davies, the silent film star and mistress to William Randolph Hearst (the newspaper magnate), this home was a monstrosity—a mansion right in the middle of the financially affluent district of Beverly Hills. With movie stars and swimming pools, one could say, "We loaded up the truck and moved to Beverly… *Hills* that is."

More than once my aunt and uncle would take us in, thank God! On her good days mom would work a little here, and a little there. When she worked, it was for upscale businesses, mostly in retail and nightclubs. Mom did not have much trouble finding employment; she simply had trouble keeping it.

Times would always improve thanks to my aunt and uncle, but they did not last—the good times never did back then. The cycle was wearisome; we would move back to the Northwest only to return to

California and then back again. Live-ins with extended family repetitively transpired throughout the ups-and-downs of mother's relationships.

Eventually, a second stepfather entered my life. My mother met him while employed at a nightclub in the Northwest. Tough as this man was, I truly came to love and respect him in many ways; he was nothing like his predecessor. He had strength and kindness underneath his rough façade. For the better part he was kind to me, and most importantly, he never physically abused my mother.

I have been told he held a championship boxing title in Hawaii for several consecutive years while serving in the U.S. Navy. At age nine, I would witness his skills when he beat the living daylights out of a man who had been pursuing my mother during one of their separations. He came home drunk to our apartment after an argument he and mother had a few days earlier, only to find another man "shacking up" with my mother. This other fellow, a relatively nice guy despite his intentions and lack of regard for his own family, ostensibly was there to protect us from my stepfather. This guy was tall and appeared to be strong in his own right, but he was no match for the champ. We had to take him to the hospital, and it was three or four days before he could remember his own name. This was the most traumatic episode I witnessed during their relationship.

Mother and I again returned to California, where she would date a wealthy physician she met while in treatment (shock therapy was really in at the time). While dating this medical practitioner, she was pursued by a twenty-two-year-old orderly from the same hospital. Fortunately, my former stepfather soon reappeared on the scene, packed up our little apartment, and returned with us to Portland. He and mother then continued to see one another periodically for two more years after their divorce. Silently I hoped for them to reconcile, as the continuous flow of random men entered and departed my mother's life.

Again I emphasize I do not relate the detail of my childhood to elicit sympathy. I have no use for sympathy. My purpose is to assist you in understanding our ability to rise above our beginnings. We are not measured by our upbringing or from where we came. Instead, we are measured by our determination to rise above our adversity and improve our lives.

At age fourteen, I found myself residing with my mother in a two-bedroom apartment in the Northwest. Though we were near family, they might as well have been a thousand miles away. Our furniture, all second hand, consisted of beds in each bedroom, a small dinette set, and a single chair in the living room. We had little because we lost much as we relocated time and again. I was fortunate to have clothes; though what clothes I did have, I had personally worked for. After attending school during the day, I would return home to find my mother had once again spent the day in bed, depressed and dependent on medication that seemed to provide her with sporadic moments of lucidness and optimism that were all too short-lived.

Such was my life. As unpleasant as it could be it was not of my own making, but just as painful, and it seemed as though it would last forever. So I prayed.

I prayed for deliverance from the chaos. I longed for a normal life with a normal family. My prayers appeared to remain unanswered and by the time I enrolled in high school, I had attended at least twenty-six schools.

I could have been described as a strange child. At least I felt as though I was different than most of the children I encountered (and I met a vast number as I relocated from school to school). Maybe all the responsibilities I endured through my mother's trials and tribulations rendered me among the most serious of my peers. I felt as though I had seen it all—much of it being beyond the comprehension of my peers. My circumstances were hard to explain to them, so I did not bother trying. I instead found myself attracted to the company of older people.

At this point I started searching for answers. Why me? Why did I have to lose my father? Why was my mother such a mess? Why couldn't I just have the normal life I desired? I was not entirely sure what normal was, but I thought it would look something like the lives of the other children I went to school with. I would eventually come to discover the "why" question is typically a poor question to ask ourselves (If this does not make sense to you now, it will by the time you have completed this book).

At age fourteen, I also read a book titled *Psycho Cybernetics,* by Dr. Maxwell Maltz. I have absolutely no recollection of how I came into possession of this outstanding book, but it was introduced at just the right time in my life. As a result of Dr. Maltz's book, I gained new insight into how our self-image is developed and how critical it is to our success throughout our lives. This insight was the beginning of a long journey for me.

I secured my first real job as a dishwasher for a fish and ale restaurant just after my fifteenth birthday. I can recall how excited I was. The free meal I was entitled to each shift excited me most because there were many times food was in short supply at home. The public assistance would run out before month's end, leaving us with little or nothing remaining in the cupboard. Believe me, I was grateful for my job, and I took pride in being the best. Within a few months I graduated to the responsibilities of head cook, supervising and maintaining the operations of the entire kitchen—a responsibility traditionally reserved for an individual much older and more experienced. I was proud of my new title. I often worked into the late hours of the night, and I took twelve-hour shifts on the weekends whenever I could get them. Though I was making a modest sum, I was contributing and I was making a difference. My promotion did have a down side: I was struggling to make school on time or some days, at all. But I needed the money, so I placed our well-being ahead of my education.

Within a year, I aspired to move onward and upward. I knocked on the door of the most prestigious retail jeweler in the community, seeking an environment that would not require me to work into the wee hours of the night. To my delight, I was hired. This new environment played a critical role in shaping my confidence and grooming me for future opportunities.

Unfortunately, by this time my faith met its end. I had given up on any remote possibility that my prayers would be answered. It was apparent I would never have the family I had asked for, and I held God personally responsible. I would soon find myself emulating the destructive patterns of my childhood environment. Outside of my work, I became reclusive and depressed. I stood at the edge of an emotional cliff, contemplating the possibility of suicide. Fortunately, I could not escape the disgust I felt for my father and the choice he had made in taking his own life.

I have met many who have suffered similar torment in their lives. You may have, at one time or another, found yourself standing on the cliff of despair, contemplating life and death. My life appeared meaningless, without purpose. I was emotionally depleted, drained of optimism and hope. My problems appeared insurmountable, and I found it extremely difficult to simply function. As I reflect, I am convinced something much greater than myself carried me through this obstacle course called adolescence. Still, it took many years for me to understand that our problems are the gateway to opportunity and the blessings we seek.

In my early adulthood I found myself feeling inadequate and isolated, with no sense of belonging. Ultimately, my survival depended on altering my state of mind, and I initially set about doing this in the wrong manner. Substance abuse was certainly among the poorer choices I made, though fortunately short-lived. At times it appeared to me that I was alone; though I have long been convinced I never was because an inner voice continually called upon me to correct my path. I believe a higher power was responsible for prompting me to ask the questions that held the key to altering the course of my life. Psychologists undoubtedly have an explanation for this, as do those who prescribe to a religious faith. I do not wish to debate the merit of either position, only to convey a concept which is very real and available to everyone who chooses to embrace it.

In my early adulthood it became evident that my career played a critical role in the development of my self-esteem. My confidence and faith rebounded, partially as a result of the constant exposure I had to training and guidance by select individuals and companies I worked for. I now know there was something far greater supporting my recovery. I began to realize my past did not equal my future. My past and all the fear, anguish, and instability associated with it were not of my making. I had just been along for the ride. I realized outside of God's influence, it is I and no other who is responsible for my life. This was my awakening and my introduction to a process that in time permitted me to disassociate myself from the role of victim I had so successfully embraced. The role of victim first appears to be comforting, only to constrain and then constrict us like a python until we find ourselves struggling for breath. I was determined to break free, determined to make something of myself, and determined my life would serve a significant purpose.

While still working in the retail jewelry industry, a customer named Robert Wiegand, who was a managing agent for Monarch Life Insurance, recruited me. As the youngest field underwriter to work for Monarch, I was licensed and selling insurance just after my twentieth birthday. I must confess I failed miserably in the insurance industry. I looked for any excuse to avoid prospecting for new business. I was terrified of rejection. I did, however, learn a great deal under the direction of Mr. Wiegand, which prepared me for opportunities to come.

I fell into opportunities more often than I can attribute to my own efforts. My forward, personable, and initially optimistic personality permitted me to find work quite easily, perhaps too easily. Consequently, the smallest opposition would justify my decision to quit, or posture my performance in such a way as to warrant my dismissal. I was duplicating the very behavior I had witnessed throughout my childhood. My mother was certainly not the most desirable role model; yet she had been the dominant influence in my life. Considerable time and a fair share of anguish passed before I would recognize the folly of my ways. I would not begin to possess the insight necessary to significantly alter this pattern until my mid-twenties.

Fortunately, the jobs I secured provided a great deal of education I might otherwise not have had, many components of which would provide the foundation for my success later in life as a trainer, coach, and consultant. I learned to sell anything and everything, and I learned from the best. I learned about commerce, economics, marketing, banking, retail, and the fundamentals of human psychology. In the years to come I acquired the knowledge and thus the confidence to play an advisory role in successfully developing and operating virtually any type of business. During this time, I was exposed to the writings of individuals such as Dr. Norman Vincent Peal, Dr. Robert Schuller, Napoleon Hill, Mark McCormack, Og Mandino, in addition to many others. I took countless courses in preparation for state and federal exams. I pursued money, security, and the possession of everything I had been denied in childhood.

Eventually those things would come, but not until I would learn how to eliminate my tendency to sabotage the very results I pursued. I would have to implement the insights and strategies of countless lessons, many of which seemed to fall short of providing me what I needed to attain my objectives. The process was trial and error. I would grasp a concept, yet countless times I would come to discover it was only part of the equation. Isolated, it was not enough. There had to be more. In the presence of discouragement and failure, despite my optimism, I would come up short and fail again. Eventually, I came to understand success resided within my failure—the success of my effort, the success of my determination, and the success of my persistence. So I continued to drive forward, energized by the hope that there was a way to live my dreams.

I recounted a snapshot of my early life to provide a foundation for the events responsible for leading me to an intimate understanding and application of what I call "Life's Critical Elements" to creating success. Believe it or not, I scratched just the surface of my challenges. In doing so, I hope my point was clear: Everyone can rise above adversity, anywhere, anytime, by believing they can, and by acting in a manner consistent with this belief.

Admittedly, I struggled. But with years of studying, real-life application, and countless adjustments along the way, I discovered the formula essential to creating lasting success. The sequence in which they are introduced may vary, but wherever success is achieved, the ingredients of the formula are present. This means you and everyone else can accomplish the extraordinary. There are no exceptions!

Unfortunately, history has demonstrated there are many wonderful discoveries, scientific developments, and spiritual insights that some have been privy to, while the rest have failed to recognize and implement them. A vast accumulation of human awareness appears to be ignored. To what can we attribute this behavior? Wouldn't you change the way you're living were you to discover a better way? I hope so, for your sake and for the betterment of everyone.

I did not create the formula I will be sharing with you. As I have said, it has always been available. I traveled the long path, paved through trial and error, to my personal discovery of its existence. I am not here to deprive you of your own journey; I am here to reveal a process that will aid you in that journey and throughout your lifetime!

When coaching, I frequently find myself referring my clients to specific books and recommending mental exercises to provide them with the greatest insight to further their progress in business and life. This book is consistent with this practice. You will be exposed to some of the most positive and accurate information I have discovered throughout my lifetime—information that will save you considerable time and resources.

The smallest decisions often lead to opportunities that far exceed our expectations. This book may at first appear to be nothing more than a small opportunity for you to advance yourself; however, I assure you it offers far more than this. This book offers you an unprecedented opportunity to discover who you really are and the purpose for which you are alive! To understand yourself and your life's purpose is a remarkable state of being in which to live.

During the thirty-plus years I have been employed or self-employed, I have worked in retail sales, banking, mortgage banking, real estate, insurance, home-improvement lines, telecommunications, advertising, radio broadcasting, and more. I have played the stock market, invested in real estate, and managed and built companies for others as well as for myself. I have made money, and I have lost money. Fortunately, I have made considerably more than I have lost and have thus provided well for my beautiful wife and our four truly amazing children. There have certainly been trials along the way—some big, some small. Regardless, we have managed well. We have a large, beautiful home and luxuries to accompany it. Most importantly, we have a strong bond in our family, with open, honest communication. At times the honesty is painful but nonetheless enlightening, and I would not have the dynamic any other way.

I marvel at my life, especially when recalling the prayer I repeated as a young man—my prayer for a normal life, with a normal family. Well, I am not certain such a thing as "normal" exists, and perhaps we would be better off not labeling what is or is not normal; nevertheless I can honestly say I am living many of my dreams!

As a personal coach I have observed what holds people back from accomplishing the things most will only dream of achieving. I have also witnessed what we can do to change the course of our lives. I can honestly tell you that whether your childhood disastrous or not, whether you consider yourself rich or poor, whether you are capable or incapable, or whether you would simply like to achieve more than you already have, you will significantly gain by reading this book and applying its principles.

Now, without further ado, I fulfill another dream of mine by sharing with you "Life's Critical Elements" to creating success. May you live your dreams!

WHAT MATTERS MOST?

Welcome to your first session with your personal coach. I recommend you read and complete one session each week over the next twelve weeks. Allow yourself time to thoroughly contemplate and assimilate the exercises outlined at the completion of each session. Begin implementing what you have learned into your daily life throughout the coming days prior to proceeding with your next session. You will find the material presented in an order conducive to establishing a foundation for promoting a rapid succession of personal victories in life as you move from one lesson to the next. The sessions simulate the type of experience you would have with a live coach, while maximizing the impact of the principles that promote an abundant life.

Some of what will be covered in the coming pages you may have already been exposed to—perhaps in a book, at a workshop, or through some life experience. Other information will be new to you, and all of it will be of benefit, both to you and to those you come in contact with. You will be asked to make commitments— the decision is yours. To achieve significant results in your life, it is essential you participate. No one else can participate for you.

Unfortunately, many of you who have picked up this book will not complete the process as outlined. Some will continue their path and wonder why life isn't providing for them as they wish. Which are you? Are you one who will complete the tasks at hand, or are you one of the many who will not? I frequently ask those who fail to follow through with a given task, where else this may be happening in their lives and how it may be affecting them.

Let me preface this session by telling you I believe there is a power much greater than what we possess alone. Some refer to it as a universal consciousness, others as a god: either way, there is something outside of us, offering direction when we choose to listen. You may be skeptical of such an assertion. Let me address the skeptic here and now. I understand where you are coming from because there was no one more skeptical of the existence of such a power than I was at one time. I have traveled the road you are traveling and can assert you are guided, even carried by a higher power. Consider the prospect: I may be right. Be open to the possibility that a higher power exists; it just might accelerate your progress.

Be Here Now

I ask you to be here now as you read this book. Remember your intention; it is to discover how you can truly live your dreams and ultimately achieve excellence in your life. Place everything else aside — your worries, frustrations, regrets, criticism, and fears. None of these things serve you positively anyway, particularly regrets and fears! It is such a waste that so many remain crucified between two thieves: the regrets of yesterday and the fears of tomorrow. Commit to make every effort to find the answers you seek, while opening your mind to the possibility that what you have believed to be true may not be. Remember, it is not what you don't know that harms you as much as the things you think you know that are untrue.

This book is a life experience that requires you to put forth effort in order to yield truly significant results. Like the coaching I conduct in person, the process requires your commitment to complete each step. (Completing all that you begin is part of the lesson.) Now let us start by seeing things as they can be, not as they appear to be!

Scarcity or Abundance?

What have you been focusing on—scarcity or abundance? There is no greater place for us to begin than with the way you *have* been thinking! One of the most powerful truths is that we attract the very thing we focus on.

"All that we are is the result of what we have thought. The mind is everything. What we think we become."—Buddha

You have met the person who worries about money and has none. His focus is on not having, and thus he deprives himself of the very thing he truly desires. To achieve anything we must see ourselves as already possessing it. Would you like to live in abundance? I am confident you would. You must begin, then, by understanding you already do, no matter how little you may otherwise currently appear to have!

"Thoughts are things." —Napoleon Hill

"Science is really nothing more than a refinement of everyday thinking." —Albert Einstein

Let us begin by looking at your present abundance. I am an American; perhaps you are as well. If you are, take a look at the following facts because they pertain to you: the United States of America comprises a little less than 5 percent of the world's population, and yet we are fortunate enough to consume 25 percent of the world's resources. Currently, 60 percent of the world's population attempts to survive on an income equal to two U.S. dollars or less per day. You likely spent two dollars at the convenience store in the past day or two without giving it a second thought!

The American Dream

Most Americans are exceptionally wealthy by world standards. Yet how often have you, your friends, family, or acquaintances complained about financial struggles? The more emphasis we place on our struggles the more we find ourselves struggling. While researching statistics for a client I discovered that a foreign-born individual relocating to the United States is four times more likely to acquire a net worth of one million dollars in his working lifetime than a natural-born citizen. How is this possible?

First, we must assess our conditioning here in America, starting with our childhood. Growing up you may have repeatedly heard, "Money doesn't grow on trees;" "We don't have the money;" "We can't afford that; we're broke;" and "The streets aren't paved with gold." ...I am sure you can think of a few more of your own.

Now take a look at what is said about America overseas: "The streets are paved with gold;" "In America anything is possible;" "Only in America;" and "America is the land of opportunity." The quality of our programming plays a major role in how we perceive reality. We act, believe, and perceive, not accordance with reality but in accordance with the truth as we perceive it to be.

Forbes magazine periodically publishes what it refers to as the "Forbes 400," a listing of America's wealthiest individuals. I remember reading a brief biography of one gentleman who made the list in the early 1980s. His name was Huang, and he was from Korea. He apparently arrived in San Francisco in 1964 with fifty dollars to his name. He established his residence in the Reno-Lake Tahoe area on the California-Nevada border, securing employment as a dishwasher with a hotel casino. Huang met a young woman from his native country, married, studied electronics, purchased a home, saved $13,000, and started a business from his garage. Sixteen years later, voilà, he was rich. At the time an individual had to possess a net worth of $200 million minimum to qualify as a candidate for the Forbes 400. Huang was worth more than one billion dollars. Some might say, "So what? Big deal. After all, this is just one guy." Yes, but he is not alone.

Take Arnold Schwarzenegger, for example. Here is a man who amassed a considerable fortune, married into one of America's most highly esteemed families, captured the imagination of the American people in numerous bodybuilding competitions, and thrilled audiences around the world with his action packed motion pictures. Arnold won people's hearts and admiration so much so that it propelled him into political office as California's governor.

Michael J. Fox is another example of an aspiring immigrant who came to the United States (from Canada) to pursue his dream. He had not even completed high school when he arrived in Hollywood, determined to make good in the film industry. He was clear about his objective and believed nothing less was acceptable!

Numerous examples exist of foreign-born citizens coming to the United States, only to exceed the average American citizen's wildest expectations. Is it possible they knew what they intended to accomplish before they even arrived? The real-life accounts are just as abundant as the opportunities which awaited them.

Are You Achieving What You Desire?

Is living anything less than your dreams acceptable to you? If it is, this book probably is not for you. On the other hand, those who desire a life filled with abundance will want to continue reading. For those who are experiencing difficulty conjuring up the motivation to read further, consider the people you love, and draw your motivation from the love you feel for them. Your success is vital to your loved ones, and it is critical to the world around you. We all benefit collectively from the success of others.

The Key Human Motivators

What pain are you currently experiencing by not having what you want? Anthony Robbins explains that the two key leading motivators in people are their desire to avoid pain and their desire to increase pleasure. Our desire to avoid pain plays the greater role of the two in the decisions we make. Having witnessed the role pain and pleasure have played in the lives of countless individuals I have coached, I can assure you most of us will not move away from our present circumstances and change until we associate greater pain with remaining as we are. This is why you will hear many former alcoholics and recovering drug addicts admit they had to hit rock bottom before they found the strength or determination to kick the habit and alter the course of their lives.

An Eye-Opening Exercise

Whether you have been exposed to something similar at one time or another, this exercise will serve a constructive purpose in preparing you to incorporate "Life's Critical Elements." Locate a writing utensil and paper. Now, permit me to take you on a rather somber journey for the next few minutes. There is method in this madness and something to be revealed about us all. Please participate. This exercise will only move you closer to your objective!

You have recently been to the doctor's office for a routine medical exam, and all appeared to be well. A week has passed when you receive a call from your physician, alerting you to an abnormality in your blood test. She asks you to come to the office so she can review the findings with you. Even more disturbing, the doctor is willing to work around your schedule and emphasizes the urgency of the meeting. You ask for additional information but she insists that you meet in person.

You soon arrive at your physician's office and are escorted promptly to where the doctor awaits you. She tells you she has some terribly unfortunate news. You are terminally ill.

"I'm sorry to be so abrupt," she says, "I have not discovered an easy way to break the news."

"What is wrong with me?" you ask her.

"You have a relatively rare blood disease — one that will rapidly deplete your energy and strength," she replies.

"How long do I have?"

"I'm not sure."

"You must have some idea."

"I don't believe it is appropriate for me to estimate, I'm so sorry," she says.

"There must be something that can be done," you fire back.

"I have consulted two specialists thus far, and I have calls into two more. Unfortunately, the physicians I have consulted concur with my findings."

You are tiring from the exchange and find yourself struggling to ask, "There must be some form of treatment. I must have some chance of survival."

"I can't say," your doctor responds. "I'm not sure what can be done as of yet. Our role will likely be to keep you as comfortable as possible."

"Comfortable? Hell! I couldn't be anymore uncomfortable than I am at this moment," you reply.

"I truly wish I could tell you I understand. To say I do would be trite at best," she says. "Let me instead offer you this thought—you face the most formidable challenge anyone can face, however, you also possess something many never will. You have time to prioritize and prepare."

"Prepare?"

"I have known patients who had no warning and no time whatsoever to do whatever was most important to them before it was too late. I suggest you take advantage of the life you have remaining."

Now, take the next minute to write down what you would do with your life if you had just six to twelve months remaining. Do so before reading any further.

1. HAVE OVER $5000 FOR MARRIAGE TRANSPORTATION
2. DO WHAT IT TAKES TO ESTABLISH SED HOLIDAY
3. GET TO IDEAL WEIGHT FOR WIFE.
4. HAVE CHILDREN
5. PREPARE CHILDREN FOR THEIR FUTURE.
6. ENJOY HOLIDAY TRADITIONS.
7. DO BEST ON GENEOLOGY AND TEMPLE WORK.
8. TRUELY HELP THE NEEDY
9. TRAVEL TO PLACES OF INTEREST

What or who came to mind? If your response is typical, you would likely spend the last months of your life with those you love, perhaps traveling in the company of someone who means everything to you. You would take time to make preparations for those you love so they would be provided for in your absence. Perhaps you would make amends with someone. These are the most common responses I encounter when conducting live workshops. Overwhelmingly, the human response is to spend time with, and prepare for the well-being, of those we love.

What prevents us from doing this now? What prevents us from making this our priority while we can? Is it time for you to prioritize your life? If not, when do you plan on doing so?

When it comes down to it, we all want the same thing — the freedom to spend more time with those we love. The fact is, we are all dying, every day. There is no guarantee as to the time we have left and yet we often approach life with little regard for this reality, all too casually taking life for granted.

Consider this: I'll bet you are more cautious with your money than you are with your time. Should someone approach you with an investment opportunity that would provide for a substantial return in six to twelve months, would you invest your money based solely on that individual's recommendation? No, not likely, particularly if you are an astute investor. You would undoubtedly request a prospectus of the venture and complete your due diligence. I hope so, or there may be little prospect of seeing your money again.

Money vs. Time

By comparison, how well do you manage your time? How much time do you waste with unproductive activities? How often do you allow others to interrupt your prioritized schedule? Do you even have a prioritized schedule? Are you clear on what you must accomplish for the day, week, month, or year?

In life we too often fail to identify our objectives, desires, or dreams, let alone begin to investigate our options, plan, and prioritize. This is exactly why so many retire with little if any financial resources to draw upon, despite the vast wealth that has passed through their hands during their so-called productive years.

Failing to Prioritize

Where have we failed? Every one of us who finds ourselves with little or no security in the golden years failed to plan and failed to take action. As the saying goes, "People don't plan to fail; they fail to plan." Perhaps we think there will always be time!

I personally have come to conclude there is accuracy in the old adage, "As we grow older, time moves faster." While I have not been presented with any scientific evidence to support this axiom, I believe there must be some truth to it, even if it is only as a result of our increased frame of reference. Our failure to plan may result from the belief that our time is limitless when the only time we have is *now*...Act on it!

Where Has Your Focus Been?

Are you where you expected to be at this point and time in life? Are you satisfied with what you have accomplished thus far? For those of you who answer no, stop and take a moment to reflect on the reasons, paying close attention to those that come to mind. Chances are your thoughts have been focused on your struggles instead of on your prize. Chances are you associate greater pain with the effort required to achieve your life's dreams than with remaining as you are. *Change your focus and you will begin to change your results.*

Give Away What You Desire

Give away what you desire, whether it is love, attention, money, or praise... and give generously. When you give without expectations, you come to understand there is far more to giving than you had thought. Those of you who have practiced this understand what I am saying. For those of you who have not experienced the significance of this principle, you have likely witnessed its power in the lives of others. Think of someone who is exceptionally generous; they always seem to have what they need or desire. *People who give receive!* They are enriched in countless ways by the joy of giving and are empowered at the deepest levels, understanding that they live surrounded by all they could want or need. Again, we attract what we focus on. *Become empowered, give what you desire, and give without expectation; it will make its way back to you, multiplied.*

For the majority of us, perhaps there is ample time to taste what life has to offer—time to learn, time to give, and time to truly live. For many even a hundred years is not enough. Personally, I desire as much adventure, knowledge, friendship, and laughter as I can fit into a lifetime. Then, were it possible, I would return for more. In the end, will you be able to say you lived as you wished? If you had just six months to live, and were you to live it passionately, you would be more fulfilled than those who live sixty years of mediocrity, trapped in a perpetual state of disappointment.

Passionate for Life

Do you awaken each day filled with enthusiasm? Do you look forward to making new friends? Do you desire to learn something you did not know before? Have you defined your dreams and risen up boldly to meet them? For those of you who cannot honestly answer yes to each of these questions most of the time, what has happened to you? Who hurt you? How long will you let your present state of mind rob you of life? You deserve more than what you are giving yourself.

You have a gift to offer the world, and it remains incomplete without your contribution. The time has come to free yourself from fear — fear of your success, fear of your failure, any fear whatsoever. Fear impedes your ability to express or create, and above all else you were designed to create. Recognize that you are happiest when you are creating, and when you are creating, you are moving closer to your potential. I assure you there is joy and prosperity in understanding this truth.

Are you having trouble getting started? Ask for help!

Embrace Your Friends

Be willing to ask for help as well as offer it. Though solitude has its place in our lives, we were not intended to bear our greatest burdens alone but rather in the company and support of others. People need people—their companionship, support, and guidance. Those around us can often see what we fail to see for ourselves. Listen and discern the advice they offer you; you just may benefit from their insight.

Be sure to choose your friends wisely; we have a tendency to take on the traits and characteristics of those who surround us. Observe their life, and determine if it mirrors the life you desire. *Choose your friends; do not let your friends choose you.*

A Sure Way to Improve Your Game

Play with someone who plays better than you. Whatever the game or profession, find another who possesses the skills you would like to emulate. Study them and learn from them; you will elevate your performance. This is true more often than not in sports and business. Use the ladder principle—one arm reaching up and the other stretching down. Just make sure your footing is strong; otherwise, you might find yourself tumbling into the very person you put forth the effort to assist.

Make certain you are climbing the right ladder, ensuring that when you reach the top you find yourself among friends. Surround yourself with an army of friends. An army of one will not as readily conquer the strongest of adversaries or overcome the most difficult of challenges as an army of many. You may not possess the skills of another, and they in turn may not possess yours, yet together you can prevail. Take off your mask and quit playing the role of the lone ranger. The risk in revealing your true identity is far outweighed by the rewards.

Get real, and get going!

Session 1 Summary

- Be here now.
- Focus on your abundance.
- Use both pain and pleasure as your ally.
- Remember what is most important to you.
- Time is more valuable than money.
- People do not plan to fail; they fail to plan.
- Observe your thinking.
- Give away what you want.
- Choose your friends carefully.
- Play with those better than you.

Your Exercises for the Week

1. Prepare a list summarizing your self-limiting or negative thoughts.
2. Describe how you have been thinking—from a position of scarcity or abundance?
3. Review your responses to the life-and-death exercise. Are you living your life in accordance with what is truly most important to you?

4. Give something to another you truly desire to possess. (Remember, there must be no expectations whatsoever.)
5. List the names of people who have hurt you at some point in your life. We will return to this later. Assess those you associate with. Do they exhibit the character you wish to develop?
6. Identify a skill you desire to improve. Find someone who possesses skills superior to your own in this area, and emulate them.

Session Review

_____
_____
_____
_____
_____
_____
_____
_____
_____
_____
_____
_____
_____
_____
_____
_____
_____
_____

EXPECT A MIRACLE

Welcome to your second session with your personnel coach. I hope you completed the exercises presented in our first session together. For those of you who have not, you would be doing yourself a disservice to continue before completing them. To truly benefit, go back to Session 1 and complete the exercises.

What Are You Settling For?

Life will give you what you ask or demand of it. We often fail to ask for what we truly want, while demanding far too little of ourselves in relationship to our potential. It is too easy for us to excuse ourselves in settling for less than what we may have otherwise felt capable of. I participated in these excuses during my early adulthood. For many years I also paid a substantial price for residing in what I refer to as the "if mentality." *If only I had done this or that. If only people were a certain way. If only this had happened. If* works against you, so do not use it!

Witness Miracles in Your Life

I have not considered myself a religious man, and yet I am a student of men who would be described as such. Religious or not, I have witnessed and benefited from miraculous events in my life, some of which transpired despite my resistance to them. For years, I failed to recognize that there was more than coincidence behind the most spectacular events of my life. When I came to understand there are no coincidences, rather the physical law of attraction at work, I began to experience a new life filled with abundance. Freed of the day-to-day fears keeping most people separated from their dreams, I found myself experiencing an increasing number of miracles, as though I could think them into existence. How exciting is that?

My Greatest Miracle

As a young man I was introduced to a beautiful young woman whose childhood bore remarkable similarities to mine. It was love at first sight. I found myself feeling as though I had known this person for a lifetime. It was as if everything I had done right to this point in my life had prepared me for her arrival. Despite my resistance to commitment at the time, I found myself emotionally devoted — hook, line, and sinker.

In no way did I believe I was financially prepared for the responsibilities of a wife and children; nonetheless, I embraced the greatest miracle of my life — my family! Ironically, I now had what I had always prayed for, but felt I was in no way prepared for it. By all accounts, I would not have described myself as one who would settle down and rise to the level of such responsibility. I can say without hesitation, my wife and children are unquestionably the greatest blessing bestowed upon me. They are my greatest miracle, born from the faith I carried as a young boy.

We Need Only Ask

Dreams do come true. History is filled with miraculous examples of what can be accomplished with a simple request. This is not to say there is no effort required beyond the asking. It is to say this is one of the ingredients to creating the outcome we seek. Eventually, I asked myself what would be possible in my life were I to accept that there were no coincidences with respect to my request of God (or the universe if you prefer) and my life experiences. Could there truly be someone or something beyond the recognizable form of creation, as we understand it? What distinguishes the granting or denial of one's request? Is anything available for the asking? Could it be God, or this power or higher consciousness, would assist me in achieving my dreams?

As a child I had been taught such an entity exists, and as a child I prayed for deliverance from the hell I described earlier. Many years passed before I recognized I had been heard. I had not been denied; rather my request was to be granted when I was ready to embrace it. Perhaps my reasoning makes sense. If it does not stay with me; it will make sense as we progress. I can tell you with complete confidence that the family I came to be blessed with is all I could have asked for, all I could have dreamed of. My family inspired something in me for the first time in my life—faith!

The Power of Faith

When we live in faith and practice forgiveness we witness miracles, large and small! Our ability to forgive and our ability to demonstrate faith are the most powerful strengths we possess. By mastering the two we bring ourselves into alignment with the light of creation. Faith and forgiveness are critical for those who seek to elevate their consciousness. We all have experienced betrayal at the hands of another, and we all have suffered persecution. We will likely experience both many times throughout our journey. *Forgive!* This does not mean we must forget the offense, for we benefit from the preservation of the lesson. It is detrimental to our success when we choose to remain fixated on the mistakes of others, and it undermines us just as much to remain obsessed with our own mistakes.

There Is No Room for Negativity

When we are free of negativity, we find ourselves free to focus on areas that will provide us with the happiness we deserve. *Positive and negative thoughts cannot occur simultaneously in our mind; we focus on one or the other.* Negative thinking blocks our creativity, eliminating our options and undermining our success. Negativity has destroyed countless dreams, possibilities, and individuals. Negativity enslaves the human spirit and assures that those who remain within its embrace will not transcend mediocrity. *To truly be free, you must first liberate yourself from your negative thinking!*

Are you ready to be free, full of light, living abundantly, and radiating with joy? Do you desire to be surrounded by positive people in the winner's circle of the human race? If so, you must replace negative thinking with positive thinking. When you do, you will have little time or desire to focus on the former.

Positive thinkers tend to believe a higher power exists. They have faith that this greater consciousness will assist them when called upon. They possess faith in what remains unseen, and in doing so they often accomplish what at first appeared to be impossible.

"Have faith in God. I assure you that whoever tells this hill to get up and throw itself in the sea and does not doubt in his heart, but believes that what he says will happen, it will be done for him. For this reason I tell you: When you pray and ask for something, believe that you have received it, and you will be given whatever you ask for. And when you stand and pray, forgive anything you may have against anyone, so that your Father in heaven will forgive the wrongs you have done." [1]

Release the Outcome in Faith

However you interpret the source, I hope you will bear with me as I elaborate on how I have come to interpret the words of Jesus as spoken above. When we pray, we are addressing a higher consciousness, whether it is within us or in the super-consciousness many refer to as God. Once we have prayed for,

---

[1] Mark 11:22, <u>Good News Bible</u>, the American Bible Society, New York, 1966.

requested, or pleaded for a specific event to transpire, we demonstrate faith by releasing the end result and focusing on our role. *We must be confident our prayers will lead to the positive outcome we seek, lest we pray in vain.* Think about this. Does it not adhere to the principle that what we focus on is what we get? Jesus clearly understood and practiced the principle of faith, as demonstrated both in his teachings and his actions. When he prayed, he prayed in gratitude for the Father having granted him that which he had asked for. (I have found only one exception to this, and in this particular instance he caught himself and deferred to the will of his Father.)

We would be wise and well rewarded to comprehend and practice this approach to life. First, it is fine to desire something constructive to transpire or materialize in your life or the life of another. I hope you will keep in mind that your request is based on your perceptions of what is good. Upon further investigation, with the passing of time and the accumulation of experience, you will often find your perceptions were limited or inaccurate. In reviewing your life and the requests you have made, you discover something different was delivered to you, better than what you had initially hoped for. You may find yourself saying aloud, "Despite my initial disappointment, I am grateful things happened as they did."

Recognize this power for what it is—a universal consciousness, an energy which sees everything as it truly is with accuracy unmatched by anything we currently understand. This power allows us to live in a life filled with harmony and purpose.

Though this power exists, so does chaos. Life is subject to both. With practice, you can ultimately determine where you reside, with purpose or with chaos. Sound a bit too philosophical or extreme? It is all part of your free will, the design that permits the human ability to create.

This brings us back to whatever we are requesting from life, God, or ourselves. Why would we pray and then question the outcome? What purpose does doubt serve? Doubt will only undermine the energy put forth to the universe, overriding the request we have made. Doubt robs us of our power, keeping us separated from the creation of what is good.

Have you ever stated with absolute confidence that something would come to pass and then made every effort to assure your declaration came true? I hope things actually came to pass as predicted. You no doubt noticed the effort and commitment you had to put forth to bring your goal to fruition. Commitment often takes on a life of its own, drawing its creator to the fulfillment of what is desired.

As you exercise faith, you will encounter new and exciting prospects in life. You will come to anticipate positive outcomes, expecting prayers and efforts to yield an abundant harvest. You will no longer worry about the outcome. Instead, you will begin to relish the process and derive as much, if not more, from your experience than the outcome you desire. This is comparable to awakening on a beautiful tranquil morning, content to be alone, basking in the silence, and anticipating the possibilities of the day to come. To possess faith is to be conscious of the existence of something far greater than yourself, a presence that loves you more than you can love yourself, and an entity that has your foremost interest at heart.

Release Your Anger

"You will not be punished for your anger; you will be punished by your anger." — Buddha

Jesus spoke of the destructive pattern we experience when we align ourselves with anger and hatred. Negative and positive thoughts cannot occupy the same space and time. You will not achieve greatest of results if you ask for something good to transpire while wishing ill of another or yourself, consciously or unconsciously. Notice I qualified the statement: The *greatest* of results. When praying for guidance or assistance in achieving your dreams or for the well-being of those you love, are you willing to settle for anything less than the greatest of results?

The longer we consume ourselves with negativity and all that can be described as such, the more we deny ourselves. Metaphysically speaking, you cannot wish ill of another without doing harm to yourself. The hatred you project is reflected back on you. Generally, who and what you attract is merely a reflection of person you are. If you want positive results, think positively. If you want the world to forgive you, then forgive the world.

You can let the past injustices you have suffered slip quietly into the distance forever. *Close your eyes after you have read this exercise, and follow my instruction*...Pull out the lists you prepared at the end of our last session. Reference the list of names of those who have hurt you along with the list of your negative thoughts. Bundle them all into one, and tie them to a large helium-filled balloon secured by a line symbolic of the choice you have made to date to hold firmly to your pain.

I have met many wonderful people who make the mistake of associating themselves with the tragedy they have experienced. It is as if they believe at some subconscious level, were they to eliminate the negativity with which they have identified, they themselves would cease to exist. Cutting the line holding the balloon represents your decision to disassociate yourself from your former fears. Cutting the line permits you to release your self-punishing behavior and your anger with yourself and with others. Cutting the line means your freedom, happiness, and peace of mind. I am not claiming it is easy to do, especially when another has truly committed an injustice against you.

Most of us have encountered someone loathsome. Although it may require considerable discipline and resolve on your behalf to let your anger go, for your sake, you must find a way. Now is as good a time as any and the sooner the better. Here and now, let the balloon go. Cut the line and feel your anger float away. The past cannot harm you further when you choose not to allow it to. You are accountable for the future you wish to create. You have the strength to release and forgive yourself, as well as others. There is nothing for you to gain by seeking vengeance, only the loss of your potential and the joy you would otherwise possess.

"Forgive them Father! They know not what they are doing!"[1]

Understand the power you have gained in the choice you have made. Feel it. There is nothing like it. This is freedom! You made the decision. It is done, and now you have made room for all you desire. I hope you will continue to act swiftly and decisively to move beyond the bondage of hatred and anger, wasting little more of your precious time.

Lift the Spirits of Others

The individual who lifts the spirit of others possesses great power. One act of kindness surpasses the value of a lifetime of criticism. The support you offer takes on a life of its own, shining with warmth and intensity, lighting the path of those who follow your example.

Why Are People So Angry?

I can recall a particular afternoon when I returned from work to be greeted by my then five-year-old daughter. As she did often, she asked how my day was. My typical response would have been, "Fine honey and how was yours?" However, for some reason, I chose to describe my frustrating day and the specific individual who had contributed to it.

---

[1] Luke 23:34, <u>Good News Bible</u>, the American Bible Society, New York, 1966.

I mentioned this individual's anger and mean-spirited behavior. I then posed a question to my daughter. She had just started kindergarten some months before, and I thought there would be benefit in her pondering the cause of people's anger. She was bound to witness it sooner than later, so I thought I might prepare her for the reality of it. I asked her if there was anyone in her class who wasn't nice — perhaps angry or mean.

Without hesitation she responded, "Yes, daddy, there is one girl who isn't very nice at all and nobody likes her!"

How sad, I thought to myself, considering the age of the child. "Why do you think people can be so angry and mean?" I asked, thinking this question would serve her sometime in the future, anticipating she would struggle to answer.

She responded without hesitation, "I believe it's because people spend more time thinking about what they don't have instead of thinking about what they do have!"

Well, there it was — the answer I had been looking for. It left me momentarily motionless. All I could do was stand there and comprehend what I had just heard. I had never before understood what this little girl had deciphered and summarized within seconds — a concise verbal description defining the human cause of anger and hostility. We spend more time thinking about what we don't have, instead of thinking about what we do have. We are thinking in scarcity rather than in abundance.

We simply cannot remain angry and hostile when we focus on our good fortune. *When we base our peace of mind on the performance of others, we are setting ourselves up for disappointment.* People will not always act as we would have them act. Accept this, and move on.

Avoid Angry People

People are often angry and mean. Love them anyway! However, that does not mean you cannot make an effort to avoid those who are habitually this way. Geographical distancing may be best with respect to some relationships.

Remember, *people are angry and mean when they spend more time thinking about what they don't have instead of thinking about what they do have.* Pay close attention to what your mind is preoccupied with.

Who Is Draining Your Vital Energy?

Observe the emotional and mental state of those around you. You may know someone close to you who is consumed by fear and immersed in chaos. Be cautious. Individuals who move from one tragedy to another often behave as if they would not know what to do were they to experience a single moment filled with peace. You will recognize the drama that provides them with a sense of purpose. They appear to thrive on conflict in their lives and in the lives of others. They are always prying ever so subtly into the lives of anyone who will permit. They are victims, and they are seeking out victims. As the old adage goes, "Misery loves company." You know exactly whom I am describing. We have all known someone, if not several people, just like this. They are asleep! They may be walking, talking, and up to mischief, appearing as though they were awake; they are not.

You will recognize them as they ramble endlessly on about the lives of others and the past injustices they themselves have experienced. They pass judgment ever so easily without restraint, while failing to consider their own imperfections. In their minds and in their conversation they relive the injustice that has befallen them. They refuse to let it go, for without it they would not know who they are; they have likely never known.

They will pull you in, eliciting your sympathy. Thus, they have justified their predicament: *I am a victim!* They have no accountability; everyone else is to blame. They are a plague to others just as they are to themselves, draining energy, optimism, and life. You may even find yourself becoming ill in their presence or shortly afterward.

"An insincere and evil friend is more to be feared than a wild beast; a wild beast may wound your body, but an evil friend will wound your mind."—Buddha

The more subtle toxicity guised in friendship is found in those "ambivalent." Heather May discussed such friends in the *Salt Lake Tribune* on June 27, 2007. Ms. May claimed we all have them: "Friends we have fun with but who also make us crazy—and maybe even sick, according to new research. They can be caring and warm, but maybe they're competitive, critical or frustrating. And depending on how we interact with them, the relationship can raise our heart rates and blood pressure, which could lead to heart disease, according to Brigham Young University of Utah researchers."

Researchers teamed up on a study published in the *Annals of Behavioral Medicine.* According to the article, "They found that when people discuss past negative events with an ambivalent friend, their health suffers. In fact, their blood pressure and heart rate rises by merely being in the presence of such friends."

The research indicates ambivalent friends aren't effective sources of support when social support is needed in times of stress. They can, in fact, be a source of stress. There is evidence for both, according to Julianne Holt-Lunstad, a BYU assistant professor of psychology and lead author of the study. "It makes you wonder, if these relationships are potentially detrimental . . . why do we have these friends?"

According to Ms. May of the *Tribune,* Holt-Lunstad "is researching that now. She has some theories on why, as she estimates it, roughly half of people's social networks include such friends. They may be relatives, co-workers, or neighbors—people who aren't easy to avoid. People who believe in the ideals of forgiveness and acceptance may be more apt to keep such friends. Plus these confidants do have their good sides. Those positive feelings for such friends may be what are causing the negative health problems. We deal easier when people we don't care about let us down than when the ones we care about do, the researcher noted. Holt-Lunstad is also studying ways to cope with ambivalent friends, by adding physical and emotional distance."

Sometimes there just isn't enough positive to offset the negative you are experiencing in a relationship. You must assess each relationship for yourself. Just remember when a friend, family member, neighbor, or colleague leaves you continually drained you should evaluate the importance of your relationship with them. Is the scale frequently imbalanced? Do not let them to drag you down. Talk with them about your concerns. A true friend will listen; if they don't, it's decision time!

Each of us possesses great value— the potential to make enormous contributions to the world. Sometimes we simply require a little outside perspective to bring us around to the truth because we are too close to recognize it for ourselves. Sometimes we need a nudge, something to rock us from our sleep—like a bolt of lightening or a meteorite.

I confess I have had my hands full a few times over the years with clients who epitomized "high maintenance," and were not ready to change. They may have intellectualized their way around to their decision to transform, but their heart was not in it. Fortunately, I have had a great deal of success overall with those I have coached, and I can confidently state that any victory begins with the commitment to succeed. So for me to agree to coach anyone, the person must demonstrate they are teachable, open to new ideas, and committed to win. I am usually able to assess this after an initial meeting or two. Still, there are instances that require more time.

Occasionally, when unable to read an individual, I may take a leap of faith, accepting their word to step out on the edge, willing to take the risk of doing something new. Nothing significant happens when we remain in our comfort zone. We must take action, and action is often synonymous with risk. Many people resist any form of risk in business or in life in general. My work parallels that of a river guide: I assist my clients through terrain laden with obstacles, except the obstacles they face are more often born of their mindset than of external circumstances. *Most of us react to the environment surrounding us rather than choosing to actively shape it.*

Trust is also a problem for the majority of people, and it all comes back to the fact that they have trouble trusting themselves. This is often true for my clients at the onset of our work. Normally resistance will not last long when acting in accordance with the values they have identified as a result of our work together. Ultimately, the results speak for themselves. Take a good look at the results. There is no better indicator of the soundness of one's judgment and efforts than the results.

I do not take credit for insights thousands of years in the making. I am simply amplifying the message of the great teachers who have identified the real universe—the one that lies within each of us. A guide does not create the topography; they are simply familiar with it. None of us can be credited for creating the laws governing our universe. Certain individuals have led us to understand how they work.

So for those of you who truly possess the heartfelt desire to achieve success and move closer to your true potential, I ask you to step forth in faith. Begin to implement the instruction I am offering so you may personally experience its merit. Once having observed the miracles soon to follow, you will begin to understand the importance of making faith your daily companion. You must stay the course. Great accomplishments take time. Eventually, you will trust yourself as you never have before. You have likely come up short in respect to achieving your dreams because you fail to trust yourself. Until you do, I am asking you to trust me.

We must begin somewhere, and our first steps in faith can be difficult, almost impossible. Faith is commonly spoken of, handed down from one generation to the next. Religious authorities pontificate the importance of faith, and we nod in recognition as though we truly comprehend. The majority does not, and the time we consume with worry proves it. It the absence of faith in our lives that leaves us struggling.

Our commitment is required long before the faintest glimpse of the solution can be recognized on the horizon. It is our inability to commit that keeps us separated from our potential.

A few years back I met a self-employed man seeking my services as a coach. I will call him Bob. Bob suffered greatly from a severe lack of confidence, something he admitted. I was quick to assess his state of scarcity. Bob's struggle with confidence, and judgment incited his disbelief and hesitation. Bob was inhibited by the potential embarrassment of making a mistake. With all of Bob's self-doubt, skepticism, and hesitation, I cannot tell you why he stepped up to the plate to swing but he did, asking for my help while still doubting my ability to assist him. I informed him that I could not be responsible for his commitments; he alone would bear this responsibility. I assured Bob he would soon be making the money required to offset any financial commitment he was about to make to me, as long as he adhered to my instruction. Still, I felt Bob's ability to meet his financial commitments would fall short unless he experienced a miracle. I was fully aware I would be part of that miracle, and I knew an opportunity would soon present itself. I was not just confident, I knew.

Perhaps you have experienced a time when you were sure something would come together. Moved by an inner voice or a strong feeling, you acted before doubt suppressed your confidence. The more we accept there is a higher power working to serve our best interest, the more relaxed we become. The more relaxed we become, the more we attract positive impressions upon our minds and ultimately the circumstances we seek.

Bob's doubt haunted him. Thankfully his temporary state of courageousness prevailed, and he agreed to proceed. We outlined our commitments and set a date to meet. Congratulating him on his decision, we shook hands and parted, ready to conduct our first session the following week. I had my work cut out for me. Among Bob's many challenges were his financial affairs. In brief, he was struggling to make money. He had purchased franchise rights to a business and was having trouble garnering new accounts. The lack of money was merely a symptom of what truly ailed him, and I knew he would be unlikely to make progress as long as he focused on his immediate needs.

Not more than a week or two into my work with Bob, I received a call from another client who knew of someone also in need of my services. The management of a retail establishment was contemplating contracting with a company representing the same line of services as Bob's. This presented an ideal opportunity for Bob. I would fulfill the advisory role required to serve the retailer indirectly as I coached and advised Bob throughout the development of his recommendations. With this being the case, the retailer would be well served and the integrity of my introduction to Bob would be intact. I scheduled a time to meet with the retailer, and then I contacted Bob, informing him of the prospective client. I do not believe the timing of this introduction was a coincidence, rather the miracle I previously anticipated.

Although surprised, Bob appeared to be delighted at the prospect of gaining a new account. As scheduled, we met with the retailer to review his needs. From my perspective there was an opportunity for all parties to benefit, and I wanted to promote Bob's confidence while simultaneously building his income. I waited for Bob to call the client to action. But he failed to recognize the customer's buying signals. I stepped in and assisted Bob in formalizing the agreement, assuring I would support him in serving his new client. This transaction was worth a great deal of money to Bob.

People frequently fail to see things as they are. It quickly became apparent Bob did not fully comprehend the meaning of what had transpired. Perhaps he simply failed to draw the parallel. Bob needed money and asked me to help him develop his skills as to better provide for his family. I told him to have faith and shortly he would have what he needed. As he moved forward with me, the universe bestowed its riches upon both of us. I never doubted something exceptional would develop. I am seldom surprised because I have come to expect it. It is amazing what is available to each of us just for the asking.

Unfortunately, Bob just could not get excited about this project and his newfound prosperity. The fact that the acquisition of new business had come together as fast as we had discussed in our initial meeting appeared to overwhelm him. I could see his mind at work, the wheels spinning as if he were searching for anything he could find to justify his skepticism and undermine any possibility for his success. I initially failed to recognize just how significant a role Bob's attitude would play in undermining his success.

In the months to come I would bear witness to Bob's emotional paralysis. Nothing was satisfactory to him. He complained about the retail account, all the work it entailed, and what "little" money he was being compensated. I cannot recall him mentioning the acquisition of new business during this time—just the feeling of futility that enveloped every area of his life. I found myself exhausted merely at the prospect of his company. It is my experience that individuals who remain emotionally paralyzed in fear will find a way to sabotage their success, if they should be so fortunate to experience it in the first place. This is exactly what Bob was doing. He began to look like a classic case of self-sabotage.

As the relationship progressed with his client, Bob failed to consult with me as he had promised. After taking it upon himself to execute a major campaign, constituting a significant portion of the client's budget and producing a dismal return, the client lost confidence in both Bob and me. I later asked Bob why he had failed to seek my assistance prior to initiating the campaign. He said he was under a great deal of pressure from the client to deliver. He also claimed his vendor had reviewed the campaign and had given him approval to move forward. I guess this is all Bob needed; he apparently felt it was unnecessary to seek my opinion. After all, Bob had heard exactly what he wanted to hear.

Ultimately, I could not come to terms with Bob's failure to consult with me (In doing so, he would not have incurred any cost.). I also found it difficult to accept his excuse that client pressure had been an issue. I was always instantly accessible and happy to accommodate both Bob and the client. After agonizing over what I should do, I terminated my coaching relationship with Bob. I believed this was my only option—not necessarily with respect to Bob but relative to my well-being. Bob had violated my trust. After all that had been accomplished in such a brief period of time, it was apparent he possessed little faith. He was asleep! I do not know if this jolted him enough to awaken him. Were Bob like many people, he blamed me and everyone else instead of accepting responsibility himself.

Bob demonstrated a moment of faith (or perhaps hope) when he enrolled to have me coach him. He undoubtedly experienced times in his life when he entertained worthiness, and those times likely inspired hope in his ability to change his condition. Unfortunately, Bob continuously reverted back to the very negativity he desired to avoid. When what he feared most came to pass, he could be heard saying, "See, I told you so. I was right all along."

Recognize the Miracles in Your Life

You may have assessed for yourself the lack of appreciation Bob demonstrated in his actions — not his lack of appreciation for my involvement, but his lack of appreciation for the small miracle we had both been blessed with. Isn't it unfortunate so many of us fail to recognize the miracles granted? I have come to expect miracles, and so I often experience them. Many have trouble believing a power will align them with the resources or solutions they seek. They fail to expect a miracle and so deprive themselves of the miracles they would otherwise experience.

Most of us know people who have had something positive happen in their lives — perhaps a series of positive events — and yet they still find something to complain about. They focus on what is not to their liking, and sure enough what was once positive in their lives has now escaped them. The majority of people suffer because they do not expect miracles. Like a child who believes anything is possible, *we must expect the miracle*. Most of us have forgotten how to do this, having become tainted by the world around us. Having failed to remain in touch with the truth we were born with, we come to doubt our worthiness and our entitlement as children of God.

Wake up! No one around you is more deserving than you are. When you decide this is the case, maybe you will quit begrudging others their success. Perhaps you will be happy for them instead, choosing to support them in their dreams and endeavors. How you perceive success and ultimately form your thoughts about success play a critical role in whether you attract or dispel it.

Be real with yourself. Think of someone you cannot stand who is successful and then ask yourself how you formulated your opinion of that person. At some level is it possible you do not particularly like the person because he makes more money than you, appears to have more than you, and may be happier than you?

After all, rich people are arrogant, rude, and self-centered, and you do not want to be one of them, right? Money may change who you are, and you are so very happy being who you are in the present moment... *Give me a break.* Can't you see the merry-go-round? Many people, somewhere along the line, came to believe that seeing themselves as worthy is to commit a sin.

I had the privilege of working with a man I met several years ago. This man believed himself worthy of the abundance he attracted, so he was a magnate for opportunity. He founded a flourishing business despite the initial challenges he faced. When he was told his company would not qualify for the financing to build and purchase the facility his business now occupies, he found a way despite the opposition. I remember the positive attitude he maintained regardless of the disappointments he faced. He never gave up. He left no stone unturned, and sure enough he achieved his objective. He expected a miracle, and when he needed one it presented itself.

This man recently shared a bit of good news with me. A prestigious clothing manufacturer had approached him, asking that he represent the manufacturer's line to retailers in a specific region, and requiring he manage his existing business in conjunction with the new opportunity. This opportunity would present an insurmountable responsibility for the average individual, but this man is anything but average. What distinguishes him above all else is his remarkable attitude, an attitude other positive people are drawn to. Like attracts like, success begets success, and the beat goes on.

It is no surprise to me that this man has since set new records in the territory he serves, and I have no doubt it is because he serves his clients so well. He practices the methods he learned during our coaching together, and his continued success serves as a testimonial to their validity. I am happy for him and those who come into contact with him because I know he will enrich their lives as they witness his faith and observe his good works. This man deserves success, and he knows it. He will always find a way to support others in their endeavors, understanding that in doing so everyone will benefit. Furthermore, I salute this man and every individual who embraces life principles of success and applies them. We are all better off for them having done so.

Expect Miracles & You Will Witness Many

I am about to share with you something so critically important to your success, your happiness, and your mental and physical well-being, that there are those who would do almost anything to prevent me from stating it. What is so frightening to those who would have this truth suppressed? The loss of their power to influence and control you is what. History has demonstrated there are those who come into power and maintain their authority through the spread of fear, the fear you may accept yourself for who you truly are...a perfect being!

You Are Perfect

It is no surprise that this will make some pause for a moment; others may even react with hostility. No bother. There is little time for those who will rant and rave when confronted with this truth. I don't care. I am sick and tired of fear-ridden, energy-draining extremists who suppress the greatness of humanity with unwarranted tirades, claiming humanity is unworthy of God. It is this kind of thinking that separates us from everything good!

While much of what we do may be imperfect, you and I as individuals are designed in perfection. I hope you will give some serious consideration to what I am saying. No one will ever match up to you. Your imagination and thinking are unique to the world. You are an original and here to fulfill a purpose no one else is meant fulfill. Despite all of your inadequacies, there is no one who will ever duplicate your potential in everyway. This is the perfection of our identity.

We are perfect in being who we are. This does not mean there isn't room for us to grow and learn to become perfect in what we do. Jesus Christ instructed the sinner to go and sin no more. He told his disciples they should do as he had done. Does this imply all of us are capable of becoming perfect in what we do? I cannot say I have ever met an individual who acted perfect in every way. Maybe I haven't looked closely enough. Perhaps my attention has been distracted by my own imperfect behavior? Perhaps if we truly believed the instruction of what an estimated one billion beings believe to be the very Son of God, we would also believe we could truly achieve perfection in what we do. Perhaps we fail to do so simply because we do not believe we can! We have been taught otherwise, perpetuating this reckless belief generation upon generation, all the while paying a dear price for the ineptitude of our spirituality. Thus again I will cite Christ's message: "Forgive them Father! They know not what they are doing!"

As I see it, Christ implied we are capable of living in perfection. We have been instructed to go forth and sin no more, not to try, but to do! I know it appears overwhelming. Regardless, shouldn't we be working toward this objective every day? How can we ever achieve excellence in anything without recognizing it is possible for us to do so?

Many of you may misinterpret perfect acts with respect to how others react to your actions. You may act in an appropriate manner, having demonstrated the greatest care with respect to a specific action, inquiry, or statement, only to discover it made another sad, even angry. Just remember sin, or imperfection in this instance, may not lie with you but with the other party. Christ witnessed this behavior repeatedly throughout his life while proposing we strive for perfection in what we do. Therein lies the possibility that we can and will.

Jesus said, "It is written in your own law that God said, you are gods. We know that what the scripture says is true forever; and God called those people gods, the people to whom his message was given. As for me, the Father chose me and sent me into the world. How, then, can you say that I blaspheme because I said that I am the Son of God?" [1]

Jesus was also quoted as saying, "The Kingdom of God does not come in such a way as to be seen. No one will say, 'Look, here it is!' or, 'There it is!' because the kingdom of God is within you." [2]

Isn't it interesting that we search outside ourselves with such fervor for something that has always existed within us? What will it take for us to accept the grandeur in which we are created, and when will we choose to live accordingly? I am referring to the individual and collective state of humanity. It will happen only when we believe it is

---

[1] John 10:34–36, Good News Bible, the American Bible Society, New York, 1966.

[2] Luke 17:20, Good News Bible, the American Bible Society, New York, 1966.

possible for us to do so. Isn't it time we began believing?

I emphasize the importance of coming to comprehend and act in accordance to this truth. Perfect actions do not guarantee a perfect response. You and I cannot control the reaction of others with respect to who we are and what we do. No matter what we do, we will not please everyone. Here again we learn from the life of Christ. Many believe he lived in a state of constant perfection; nonetheless, he made many people angry—to the point that he was hated and killed. Those who hated him were threatened by his claim to be the perfect Son of God and by his challenge to the conventional authority of the time. He threatened the power base of the very religion in which he was raised. The threat was his honesty and his acknowledgement of his greatness, your greatness, and my greatness.

Widely accepted theological accounts of Jesus' life indicate he honored the commandments, and lived so he might fulfill the will of his Father; yet many of his own people turned against him. He instructed generations past and future that we are gods, and we could do as he had done. Is it possible that we can live in perfect harmony with the laws of our universe? There is a strong probability that it all comes back to what we perceive to be true. Should we believe it impossible for us to live in such a way, then it is certain to remain so.

Had all of humanity believed we could never fly, we would not be flying today. The same is true for much of what we have achieved, despite the fear and skepticism of the masses. Much of what we take for granted today was deemed impossible just a few generations ago. Any of us can play a perfect game at one point in time. Should we begin to believe we could play a perfect game, would we witness more of humanity aspiring to play the perfect game? The bar will not be raised unless we make the effort, and we generally fail to make the effort unless we first believe it to be possible. It is pretty simple when you put it all together: Everything we do or don't do, well or poorly, has to do with how we think.

I am not asking you to accept my interpretation. You may find it difficult to believe an individual, or humanity in general, could achieve a state of perfection. I am asking you to question how you have come to this conclusion. How and when did your belief system originate? Better yet, what is your definition of perfection? Some may respond that to live in perfection we must be flawless. Now, are we talking about a state of perfection or acting perfectly?

A state of perfection as described by many may include perfect health, a perfect emotional state, perfect appearance, perfect relationships, financial abundance, and a perfect spiritual state. This is not the perfection I am speaking of. I am referring to being at peace with who we are, and striving for excellence in all we do. There will always be someone who we perceive to be superior in some way to ourselves, and this is okay. Rather than comparing yourself to others or envying them, decide to be the best you can be in whatever you desire to accomplish. In doing so, you will discover perfection in being who you are.

"The quality of a person's life is in direct proportion to their commitment to excellence, regardless of their chosen field of endeavor." — Vince Lombardi

For those who may simply find it unacceptable to even contemplate the possibility of achieving perfection in anything, they may instead choose to strive to achieve excellence.

"We are what we repeatedly do. Excellence, then, is not an act, but a habit." — Aristotle

Free Will Determines Identity

I was recently asked why God allows bad things to happen. The individual who asked this question was referencing a disaster of epic proportions. You likely recall the horrific loss of life resulting from the 2005 tsunamis, one of the most catastrophic events of recent human history. We found ourselves helpless with respect to preventing it. Or were we truly helpless? To what degree did our free will play in failing to prevent the enormous loss of life? Rather than ask why God would let such tragedies befall humanity, we would be better to ask what humanity could do to prevent them.

With our free will comes responsibility, whether we like it or not. This is why so many willingly and readily pass the responsibility to others, especially God. When they find themselves backed into a corner, ill prepared for what has befallen them, they cry out to God, failing to remember or acknowledge how they got there in the first place. Worse yet, they tend to do this repeatedly, falling short of understanding their behavior and correcting their ways. Again, Christ's comprehension of the human frailty is applicable: we know not what we do.

Unfortunately, despite our common inability to step up and take responsibility for the mess we have created, we remain blessed with our free will. Our free will exists so we may exist. The "I am" and our ability to determine what this will be, distinguishes our existence. Without this we would fail to exist.

I look forward to some point in the not-to-distant future, when humankind will grow up and quit blaming God. God's perspective is far more encompassing than many individuals credit. God has little to do with tragedy, other than the design that permits good to prevail in the aftermath. There is a natural cycle to life; it can be brutal, unforgiving, kind, and generous. Regardless of the hand we are dealt, we must play it the best we can, making the most of the opportunities we have.

Bad things happen. Fortunately for us, we can create something good of the bad by making the right choices. In tragedy there exits the opportunity for good to triumph. Again, it is our will that determines whether this will be the case. It is also important to note that many tragedies can be prevented by making the right choices in advance. For example, the tsunamis would not have been a tragedy of such magnitude had there not been the loss of life. Monstrous waves simply would have caused some serious property damage. The subsequent reconstruction would have demanded a united effort, created new jobs and prosperity would have prevailed.

The tragic truth is we could have prevented much of the loss of human life and suffering, had it been our priority. Early-warning systems exist. Despite the technology, we failed to implement them. The decision was likely financially motivated. Ultimately, we found ourselves laboring frantically to rescue the injured, and we raised billions of dollars in an attempt to fix what we could have prevented with millions of dollars. Unfortunately, we failed those who perished, and we can never begin to erase the pain and suffering of those injured or those who lost their loved ones; however we could have prevented it in the first place. The collective will to do so would have made all the difference.

Currently, nations spend vast sums of their economic wealth daily to posture themselves militarily. We go to considerable lengths to defend ourselves from one another and place far less emphasis in responding to the unpredictability and potential hostility of our natural environment. As a result we often find ourselves unprepared when Mother Earth assumes the role of adversary.

We Control More Than We Think

The scarcity of money is not the problem. The problem lies in our thinking and in our priorities. We possess the free will to determine what our priorities are, and we would have certainly saved tens of thousands of lives had we redefined our priorities and redirected our resources. We failed to implement our technology, and those who perished failed to draw upon the instincts inherent in each of us. Ironically, the more advanced we become technologically, the more we appear to distance ourselves from our intuition and the wisdom of our ancestors.

Countless animals fled the beaches well before the ocean made its way inland. At least one group of people did as well. A tribal community modern civilization would categorize as primitive, known as the Onge (OHN-ghee), survived while so many perished. As tourists in Thailand enjoyed a morning swim in receding waters and fishermen in Sri Lanka ran out to pick up flopping fish stranded on the exposed seabed, the Onge fled to higher ground. Apparently the Onge understood the disappearing water meant danger.

Were someone to be outside looking in, they might conclude contemporary minds have become so cluttered that our instincts have been displaced, or perhaps we have failed to heed the lessons passed down from prior generations. For many of us, the valuable senses that have preserved our species throughout the millennia of human existence are little more than a sentiment. Has humanity, then, been relieved of it senses?

It is obvious we do not possess the understanding or technology to control much of the environmental conditions which threaten us. We can, however, opt to utilize the resources we have to preserve human life wherever and whenever possible. At present it does not appear as though this is a priority. Unfortunately the tsunamis of 2005 did not promote a greater unity among people and nations. Instead, we watch as nations continue to battle for the Earth's resources while governments choose to protect industry that abuses the planet. It is absolute insanity. We are better than this—far more magnificent than our actions would demonstrate. Regardless, it is not what we contemplate but what we do that defines us. Ultimately, our will prevails over God's will. After all, free will is his gift to us. Who, then, is responsible for what ails us?

Accepting Responsibility

We have far more influence over our fate than we credit ourselves, both as individuals and as a society. We are only limited by our imagination. With time and persistence, we collectively possess the ability to accomplish almost anything we aspire to. Some of what we initiate may take generations to complete. For the betterment and continuance of our race, hadn't we best begin to perceive the grander perspective of what we do today and how it affects coming generations?

When we stretch the human imagination, we discover the mind's propensity for creation. As we make new personal discoveries and find ourselves stretching far beyond the boundaries that once confined us, we find a new enthusiasm for life. Born again in spirit, our attitude is reshaped, renewed, and relit with the desire to make a difference. We seek to enlighten others so that they may break free from their self-imposed suffering and rise with us to new heights of awareness. We wish they too could be free of the ignorance and fear that binds them—that they could see their life and this world as it can be.

Be cautious. Not everyone is ready to receive this good news, and you might find yourself exhausted from your efforts to share. We are all more vulnerable to the negativity and cynicism of the world when we are fatigued. Nothing will drain us of enthusiasm, passion, and energy faster than negative acquaintances. Be at peace, take your time, and garner your strength, understanding their teacher will appear when they are ready.

Session 2 Summary
- Live in faith, expecting a miracle.
- Rid yourself of negativity.
- Forgive others, and forgive yourself.
- Come to terms with who you are and in whose likeness you have been created.
- The kingdom of God is within you. Raise the bar with respect to your expectations.
- Fear neither life nor death.
- Make room in your life for what you desire.
- Avoid angry people.
- Recognize your miracles.
- Let your perfection prevail.
- Strive for excellence in all you do.

Your Exercises for the Week
1. Prepare a list of the miracles in your life.
2. Prepare a list of miracles you have wished for.
3. Review the balloon exercise. If you did not complete it, do so now.
4. Clean your mind and your home of clutter. Make room for your coming blessings. Select something you have always wanted to improve and begin.

5. Do something you enjoyed as a child, preferably something you have not done for a long time.

Session Review

_____
_____
_____
_____
_____
_____
_____
_____
_____
_____
_____
_____
_____
_____
_____
_____
_____
_____
_____
_____
_____
_____
_____
_____
_____
_____
_____
_____
_____

KNOW THYSELF

Welcome to Session Three with your personal coach. By now, you are expecting me to ask whether you have completed the exercises from Session Two. For those of you who have, it's time to continue; for those who have not, get going. Obviously, the choice is yours.

One critical question in determining our life's course has perplexed the majority of human beings since the beginning of time: Who am I? Take a moment and ponder this question. How would you define yourself? Many people begin by reciting what roles they fulfill: mother, father, homemaker, or professional. We frequently associate ourselves with our names, titles, and occupations. Does this define your identity, or does it define the role you play in your daily life?

Take a moment to write down ten characteristics you like about yourself. This exercise is worth far more than the effort required, so write them down before you proceed further.

1. _____
2. _____
3. _____
4. _____
5. _____
6. _____
7. _____

8. _____

9. _____

10. _____

How did you do? If you could easily think of three positive qualities without struggling, I commend you. Based on my experience, you represent the minority. Now write down ten areas you could improve upon. Do it now.

1. _____

2. _____

3. _____

4. _____

5. _____

6. _____

7. _____

8. _____

9. _____

10. _____

Did you find it easier to identify personal characteristics you find less flattering about yourself? Unfortunately, most do. What does this tell us about ourselves?

How We Come to Perceive Ourselves

It is likely no surprise that many of our personal perceptions are developed at a young age. I recall an experience that played out repeatedly during my childhood undermining my self-esteem then and for some time thereafter. As I relocated from school to school, I struggled with my studies, often finding

myself behind in a subject or having had no exposure to a subject whatsoever. As you might imagine, the affect was devastating at times — high anxiety and low scores are a miserable combination for anyone. And my mother was anything but supportive.
I remember her telling me I was stupid, undisciplined, and would never amount to anything!

You will find there is little credibility with respect to many of the negative perceptions you may have about yourself when you invest the time to assess the source. I remember my daughter returning home from school one day to inform her mother that a fellow student had been reprimanded during class for poor behavior. The teacher informed the student, in front of her peers no less, that she was the worst student she had taught in all her years. Wow! There's one for you. Imagine the affect on this child.

You may have had an experience similar to this. Take a moment to draw upon your own childhood memories. What beliefs have you internalized that originated from the opinion of others? Consider the source and their motive. Forgive them, let it go, and move on. Or you can opt for years of therapy. The choice is yours.

Overcoming Negative Self-Perceptions

It has long been apparent to me that my mother projected her own feelings of inadequacy and frustration when expressing her disappointment in me. I would have benefited in recognizing this in my early years; it certainly would have saved me considerable grief. The problem is that I didn't. I thought something was in fact wrong with me, and it would require years to come to terms with this false perception. Fortunately, I met some wonderful people through the years, their insight and guidance positively affected my life. In time, I transcended my negative views by identifying their origin and weighing the credibility of the source. I assure you this can be done. You will accomplish what you want when you choose to put aside your false perceptions admitting there is no rationality behind them.

A great place to begin is in recognizing that most of us react emotionally to our environment. When we step back and look at our situation from a third-party perspective, we discover we are more likely to behave rationally and make better decisions. Fatigue, like fear, often plays a critical role in determining how we react to a particular circumstance. Discipline also plays a vital role. The majority of us fall short of being the most disciplined as possible.

I received some good advice many years ago when a friend and supervisor suggested I make important decisions on an up day, not when I was feeling defeated. We often make critical decisions when we are tired, burned-out, and depressed. What a terrible time to trust our judgment! Hold off on important decisions. Make sure you are rested. A day can make all the difference in your perspective, and a little patience can save you a great deal of misery.

Simple Choices Make a Difference

I recall a client who struggled with anxiety whenever he was in the presence of his company's CEO, which occurred often because he was in upper management. I asked "Jack" what he thought was contributing to his discomfort when in the presence of this individual. He said the man could be exceptionally intimidating. I asked Jack to evaluate his own qualifications. After doing so, he said he could not find any reasonable explanation for his feelings of inadequacy. Qualified for the position he held, he was dedicated to his work, and desired to perform to the best of his ability. He agreed there was little, if any, justification for his anxiety.

I offered him some leverage, assuring him many people were as concerned with his opinion of them as he was with their opinion of him. I told him that were he to continue down this path, he would eventually undermine his relationship with the company's CEO. I then encouraged Jack to quit being intimidated in the presence of others. He questioned whether it was that simple. I guaranteed him it was.

We often make decisions about ourselves and the world around us based on false perceptions, buying into another's opinion of us and what we may or may not be capable of. When we find a decision holding us back, we should reassess our position. It is irrational to think we cannot recreate ourselves when we have permitted others to form our perception of the world and who we are. You have likely reacted to life based upon perceptions instilled at an early age. In reality, they may have no basis regarding who you truly are or what you are actually capable of; yet they may work against you every day, as though you were operating on autopilot. All you have to do is recognize this, and then choose to take back control of your life.

Control Over Our Minds

"Jack" assessed the price he was paying for his thinking. He recognized his behavior was inhibiting his advancement within the company. He realized there was greater discomfort in denying himself the future he deserved than in forging ahead with his relationships, personal and professional. I asked him how long he was willing to sacrifice his income, advancement opportunities, and peace of mind. He sat silent for a moment and pondered my question. Then he asked me once again, "Is it really this easy?" I told him, "Yes, when you choose for it to be."

I knew Jack was exceptionally intelligent, and the rationale of my instruction would appeal to him. Then and there, with the recognition of this simple truth, Jack's face illuminated. He knew he could shed his anxiety by simply choosing to do so. Jack had decided to decide. He began thinking and acting in a manner far more conducive to his success. Within weeks, his confidence increased significantly.

"It is better to conquer yourself than to win a thousand battles. Then the victory is yours. It cannot be taken from you, not by angels or by demons, heaven or hell." — Buddha

The Core of the Matter

Most of us have felt uncomfortable in the presence of others. Drawing upon your personal experience, identify a situation or relationship that made you uncomfortable. What made you uncomfortable? Did you find yourself fighting feelings of inadequacy? Consider whether your feelings were justified or whether you were behaving based on false perceptions. Were you crediting yourself for the talents, knowledge, and experience you possess? Most people do not give themselves the credit they deserve.

You must believe in yourself for others to believe in you. Self-doubt is transparent to those around you. When you doubt yourself signals of doubt, though often subtle, are apparent in your mannerisms, speech, and expressions. Take note of this and observe the way you act in the presence of others. Do you convey confidence, or do your insecurities speak volumes? What is the cost associated with your present behavior, and how long are you willing to pay this price? What benefits could you derive by deciding to change your false perceptions? It really is as simple as making a decision to change. Remember, your present thinking is based on previous decisions you have made about yourself and the world around you.

Of course, an endless stream of influences from parents, peers, and strangers alike, can affect how we perceive ourselves; however, we cannot escape the reality that *we decide* who we are and how we will behave. As I have stated, many of our beliefs are instilled at an early age. Now is a great time to shed any belief system holding you back from the life you desire. You are no longer a child! The maturity you possess allows you to accurately assess your perceptions. You can choose to eliminate those working against you; it is as easy as making the decision to do so. The process will not necessarily be free from discomfort. You could, in fact, experience a great deal of discomfort. Remember, "No pain, no gain."

The following exercise is a great way to gather insight into who you really are and whether your present ambitions compliment your true identity.

List the names of three individuals you admire. Write one word next to their name that best describes the characteristics you admire most about them.

1. _____
2. _____
3. _____

What did you come up with? Take a good look at the words you used to describe the character of the people you named. There is a strong probability you identify with the qualities you attributed to these individuals. You have most likely listed attributes that comprise your own core identity. By identifying the qualities in a person we admire, we may determine whether our aspirations are in conflict or in harmony with who we are at a core level. When you find yourself in conflict, you will want to reassess your present objectives and determine if they truly deserve your attention, let alone your time and resources.

Do not be surprised should you find yourself reevaluating what you once perceived as important only to discover it does not really align with who you are. After completing this exercise, many people identify something they currently do that they have falsely been led to believe would make them happy. With this discovery they understand their conflict and the reasons for their discontent. This is a big step toward aligning their behavior with their core identity.

When we choose to pursue interests or act in a manner complementary to our core identity, we will achieve our primary objectives with greater ease and find ourselves much happier with the results. Some people, although having clearly identified their objectives, still find themselves paralyzed by fear, avoiding any act that may remotely provide for the possibility of their success. "What if I fail?" they ask. I have posed this question countless times myself, subject to the same internal voice of doubt in my own ability to get the job done. When this is the case, I defer to the instruction of Vincent Van Gogh: "If you hear a voice within you say 'you cannot paint,' then by all means paint and the voice will be silenced." Or I reference the insight of William Shakespeare: "Our doubts are traitors, and make us lose the good we oft might win, by fearing to attempt." You may also appreciate the more modern interpretation by Nike: "Just do it."

Make the conscious decision to do whatever it is you have always dreamed of doing! *Decide to decide.*

Recognize the paralysis associated with your present thinking. The costs are far too high for you to remain motionless, pressed by the fear of an undesired outcome. It is truly better to have attempted and failed than to have failed to make an attempt. Should you find yourself thinking negatively, heed the advice of Dr. Norman Vincent Peale: "Change your thoughts, and you change your world!"

Pay Attention to the Words You Use

There comes a time when many people concede it is time to act. They conjure up the courage to give it the old, "I'll try!" What visual image of success does this inspire? Absolutely none; instead, it implies they may not succeed at all. We will discuss the power of visualization and how it relates to communication in the coming session. For the time being, I recommend you eliminate the word *try* from your vocabulary; it serves little or no constructive purpose. You are not a little train struggling up the mountainside repeating, "I think I can, I think I can." You can! It is time you replace "I'll try" with "I'll do it." Avoid words that fail to inspire confidence—this includes self-talk.

Creating an Empowered Mindset

I spoke earlier of my stepfather—the boxer who held title during his tour in the Navy. I used to say to him, "Dad, what if we were to do this or if we were to do that, wouldn't this happen?" And so on. The point is I used the word *if* frequently, to which he would respond, "If a cow shit butter, you wouldn't have to churn." This may sound harsh, yet he made a valid point. When we say to ourselves, "If only this would happen," we imply that we have little or no influence relating to the circumstances created. Does this promote an empowering or disempowering state of mind? From which state would you prefer to manage your life? Once appearing as nothing more than a cynical response to a child's inquiry, my stepfather's sarcasm gained new light shortly after his death.

Driving home one afternoon, I heard a song by the recording artist Roger Whitaker, a Canadian folk singer I was familiar with thanks to my stepfather. The song's message is one I have come to appreciate:

> *Now if you load your rifle right*
> *And if you fix your bayonet so,*
> *And if you kill that man, my friend,*
> *The one we've called a foe,*
> *And if you do it often lad,*
> *And if you do it right,*
> *You'll be a hero overnight,*
> *You'll save your country from a fight.*
> *Remember, God is always right,*
> *If you survive to see the sight,*
> *A friend now greeting foe.*
> *No, you won't believe in if any more,*
> *It is an illusion, it is for children!*
> *No, you won't believe in if any more.*

My stepfather had come to understand the harm in surrendering our empowerment to *if.* Eliminate *if* and *try* from your vocabulary, if possible. Give it a go anyway! Forgive me— I am having a little fun with this. My point is you can empower yourself by using words that evoke faith and accountability.

Now it is time to ask yourself some of the most important questions of your life:

- **Who are you?**
- **What do you desire?**
- **Who do you desire to be?**
- **What do you desire to accomplish?**

_____

_____

_____

_____

_____

_____

_____

_____

_____

_____

This exercise will culminate in providing you with what I refer to as your *"Personality Identity Declaration."*

Personal Identity Declaration

You are most likely familiar with what a mission statement is and its importance in defining the purpose or intent of a business. Well, what about a personal mission statement? What is good for business can be just as good for the individual, don't you think? I know so, and I recommend you take the time to write a Personal Identity Declaration, which will define *your* life's purpose and your character values. Focus on the process of growing toward your desires, while realizing one way or another, you possess the means to achieve what you choose to accomplish. Far more gratification comes from recognizing this than actually possessing what you desired in the first place. Remember the joy we experience is in the journey as much as it is in the destination.

Refer to the three individuals you listed and the characteristics you identified. Start with the characteristics you admired in them, using this as your foundation to construct your personal statement. This is yours and yours alone. Be creative and have fun.

Personal Identity Declaration:

_____

_____

_____

_____

_____

_____

_____

Champions Rise Despite Adversity

Champions are distinguished by their determination to rise again and again despite criticism, opposition, and fatigue. When you behave like a champion, you will ultimately be embraced for your courage and determination. We do embrace courageous people, don't we? We even find ourselves in awe of their feats, status, and wealth. At times we may idolize champions, if only because we understand they have somehow broken free from the grip of what can be a puritanical, hypocritical, and repressive world—a world that tells us to watch ourselves, not to get too big for our britches, be seen and not heard, and so forth. You know exactly what I am talking about.

I can think of a couple of show-offs millions of us have come to love: actors Robin Williams, who I understand was voted in high school least likely to succeed; and Jim Carey, who makes twenty million dollars per film. There are many examples of those who have defied mediocrity. The question is do you count yourself among them?

What Is Holding You Back?

What incites us to restrain others and ourselves with such fervor? We emulate the behavior of crabs, pulling our peers back into the abyss of mediocrity just as they are breaking free of their restraints. What gratification do we receive in holding another back from greatness? Do we find it consoling to witness another's failure? Or sadly, perhaps we think this permits us to justify our own.

Suppressing Your Potential

Scientists say we use a small portion of our mind's capability. When we raise the bar, we will discover our suppressed potential, both collectively and individually. The result will likely mirror what we witnessed athletically when the barrier of the four-minute mile was broken—another record was set soon afterward. We will discover, as our ancestors did, that we will not fall from the edge of the Earth when we venture beyond what we currently understand; rather, we will expand beyond our present boundaries once again.

Few deserve to be credited for their courage — the rest ride the tide set in motion by those who dared to challenge the confines of traditional thinking. Thank heavens for them; they set the bar and represent the greater potential of humankind. We live amidst the convenience of their technology: we drive the cars they envisioned; we read by the light they conceived; and we extend our lives with the medicine they developed.

What would you do were you unstoppable? What would you do were you to recognize that you are as capable as those I have described? What would you do as a perfect child of God? Take note of the possibilities. Write them down, and then proceed.

Encountering the Crabs

Perhaps at one time you have taken aim at the stars while those around you deemed you crazy. Good! Let your inspiration overshadow the fearful ranting of the doomsayers who would predict your demise. Take action and emulate the likes of Walt Disney. Disney's judgment was questioned when he aspired to build a theme park in the midst of orange groves more than fifty miles from Los Angeles. "The public will never drive that far," his critics cried. The rest, as they say, is history!

"What the mind of man can conceive and believe, it can achieve." —Napoleon Hill

Rising Above the Opinion of Others

Dr. Robert Schuller is a man you may well want to emulate. My wife introduced me to Dr. Schuller's writings almost twenty years ago. Dr. Schuller arrived in Orange County, California, in the mid-1950s, assigned by his church to build a cathedral. He established a ministry within walking distance of what was to become Disneyland. From the modest beginnings of preaching at a drive-in theater rooftop to the present-day sermons in the architecturally renowned Crystal Cathedral, Dr. Schuller has motivated millions worldwide with his message of "Positive Christianity," rewarding his listeners with lesson upon thought-provoking lesson.

Dr. Schuller frequently speaks of human victories inspired by faith. Weekly, the *Hour of Power* televised broadcast is viewed around the world, introducing its viewers to champions who bear testimony to the power of positive thinking. A student of such great men as Dr. Norman Vincent Peal and Dr. Victor Frankel, Dr. Schuller is a true possibility thinker, dreamer, and doer. He attributes much, if not all of his success to prayer and faith, accompanied by their complementary ally, action.

We can learn much from individuals like Dr. Schuller, Disney, Edison, Franklin, Ford, and the like. Remember, we have a strong tendency to take on the characteristics of those who surround us. Who are you associating with, and as Dr. Phil would ask, "How is it working for you?"

Facing Opposition and Discouragement

Dr. Schuller tells a story of the time, while attending seminary, that a professor critiqued his literary skills, leaving him discouraged. Evidently, a writer in the making he was not. Nonetheless, the time came when Dr. Schuller would be called upon to write for an Orange County newspaper at the request of the publishing editor. Schuller accepted the assignment despite his reservations, and his subsequent articles provided material for his first book. When we hear a voice within us say we cannot write—or do something else—then we by all means should write until the voice is silenced. Dr. Schuller has written thirty-six books to date.

Exercise Your Imagination

What are your dreams? Are they truly yours, or have you taken on the dreams of another? Who may be discouraging you? Perhaps you aspire to be something other than what your parents, peers, educators, church, or culture have encouraged you to be. What would you choose to have happen in your life, and does it align with your core identity and values? Give a little thought now as to *how* you would accomplish your desires. When you have prepared a place for your dreams to become reality, they will become reality.

Einstein said imagination is more important than knowledge. We all posses imagination, and as it is often repressed by the surrounding world, we frequently fail to exercise it. Remember when you created an imaginary world of wonder as a child? When did you last permit this old friend to accompany you through your day? Do you recall the endless possibilities inspired by this creative companion? If you are like the majority, you have set your imagination aside, mistaking it as childish. In doing so, you think you have become pragmatic and wise. I challenge you to consider that you have instead lost yourself and all that really ever mattered. You know I am speaking truthfully; you feel it. You have settled for something other than that to which you truly aspire. After all, it was unrealistic and most certainly unobtainable. I too am guilty of putting childish things aside, and I know the pain of doing so.

Life is too short for you or me to waste. When we were children we played until exhausted, and then soon returned for more. We dreamed of doing great things, being surrounded by fascinating people, traveling to faraway places. Some of us were so bold as to believe we would change the world. Do you remember?

There will never be a better time than the present to rekindle your relationship with your imagination. What will you do now after realizing you are unstoppable? You may not yet be convinced you are unstoppable—the adult in you remains fixated on what you perceive to be your reality. Imagine your dreams are possible. What will you do?

There is no need to presently know just how you are going to accomplish the goals you have identified. Do not attempt to qualify the feasibility of your undertaking now. The answers will come; you will be introduced to them in good time. The greatest wisdom is contained within the questions you ask rather than the answers you seek.

Faith Moves Mountains

The only way to actually understand faith is to live in it! That's right. Live your life in faith and you will never hesitate to commit to what the majority would describe as impossible. For those of you who profess to believe in God, I challenge you to quit talking about faith and begin living it. This means stretching yourself beyond what you perceive as possible and understanding that nothing is too big for God. Faith is what you will demonstrate when you commit to the impossible, as you see it, with little regard as to how it may be accomplished. This is among the most difficult of all obstacles for us to overcome, and yet the simple act of commitment opens the door to accomplishing the impossible.

"If you have faith as big as a mustard seed, you can say to this hill, go from here to there and it will go. You could do anything." [1]

---

[1] **Matthew 17:20, <u>Good News Bible</u>**, the American Bible Society, New York, 1966.

Now is a good time for us to conduct another exercise. Reference your Personal Identity Declaration and the list of things you will accomplish now that you recognize you are unstoppable. Note your present performance in various areas of your life compared with these two lists. Using a scale of one to five (1 = poor, 2 = fair, 3 = good, 4 = very good, 5 = excellent), how do you rate yourself in the following?

For those of you contemplating skipping this exercise, consider why you started reading this book in the first place. If you think you can do this without some serious effort, you are sadly mistaken. For those of you committed to creating a better life, do the very best to provide yourself with a balanced assessment, understanding your greatest strengths may pose the greatest threat to undermining the harmonious life you desire. The reason for this should become clear to you in our tenth session together. (**See heading: Understanding the personality traits that drive us).**

Additionally, permit yourself the tolerance you would offer a friend. Be encouraged and applaud yourself for investing the time to reflect upon and assess the attributes that make up the individual you are. Recognize the growth you are experiencing by completing this process. Though it may be difficult for many, in completing this exercise we come to understand, perhaps for the first time, the areas of our lives deserving the most attention.

Rate Yourself on the Following:

	Present	Desired
1. Good physical condition	3	5
15. Ability to deal well with stress	4	5
4. High energy level	2	5
12. Positive attitude	3	5
5. Relationship with significant other	4	5
6. Relationships with children	2	5
17. Relationships with business associates	2	5
19. Relationships with employees	4	5
16. Relationship with employer	2	5
10. Adequate time to rest	5	5
7. Healthy financial status	1	5

2. Healthy self-esteem   _4_   _5_

13. Passion for your work   _5_   _5_

3. Satisfaction with life   _3_   _5_

8. Accomplishments   _3_   _5_

9. Ability to deal
   well with conflict   _2_   _5_

1. Spirituality and
   Intimacy   _4_   _5_

     Which of these areas is of the greatest priority to you? Number them one to eighteen, with one being the most important. Upon completion, review the session summary and finish the summary exercises. For those of you who desire instant gratification, stay the course. Until then, live in faith!

Session 3 Summary
- Who are you?
- You have the power to overcome a negative self-image — decide to decide.
- You have control over your mind.
- What is your core identity?
- Use empowering words.
- Champions rise above adversity.
- Exercise your imagination.
- Where can you improve?

Your Exercises for the Week

1. Identify and list your negative self-perceptions.
2. Pay close attention to the words you are using.
3. Review your core identity and reference it frequently.
4. Identify and list who and what you have permitted to hold you back.
5. *Exercise* your imagination.
6. Complete the performance questionnaire and then prioritize by importance.
7. Determine the level to which you wish to adjust your future performance.
8. Describe in writing what you desire to be, have, create, and accomplish in life (your Personal Identity Statement).

Session Review

_____

_____

_____

_____

_____

_____

_____

_____

_____

_____

_____

_____

_____

_____

_____

SESSION 4
IMITATE THE MASTERS

Welcome to Session Four with your personal coach. By coming this far you have demonstrated you are serious, you want more out of life, and you are willing to work for it. I commend you! Some readers began this book with good intentions; however, they soon discovered it involved far more effort than anticipated. They set it aside and will likely fail to complete it. Where else is this happening in their lives? Unfortunately, it is undoubtedly affecting them in many areas, personally and professionally. I emphasize this because I want you to recognize yourself for the effort you are putting forth. You have confirmed you possess an essential quality aptly attributed to those who are successful; you are tenacious when pursuing your goals. Fantastic! We will accomplish a great deal together!

Dream the Impossible Dream

Some of you may recall a time when you were accused of being a dreamer, as if the title designated you as unrealistic, irresponsible, and incapable of adjusting to or accepting reality. The fact is, those who have dared to dream, those who have embraced their dissatisfaction with things as they are, those who have challenged the status quo, and those who have sought innovative options permitting themselves to redefine their limitations have accomplished the most remarkable feats known to humanity. I invite you to join them. *Take the road less traveled, for it will make all the difference.*

Where would we be if not for the daydreamers? What would our modern world look like if they had failed to dream? Now, before the cynics go off on a tangent citing all that is wrong with our day, I remind you that every period of recorded history has faced its struggles. Though we continue to thrash about in our pursuit to create a better world, we do so thanks to a small number of creative thinkers — those who have toiled, labored, struggled, and died at the hands of tyrants; it is they who pave the way for future generations.

Allow yourself to dream. Everything worth possessing began with a dream — a dream which led to a vision, a vision inspiring the beneficiary into motion, promoting action resulting in some constructive form of creation. History repeatedly demonstrates the constructive nature of daydreaming. Instead of reprimanding our children in class for daydreaming, we should incorporate a curriculum teaching them to harness their creativity. We should allocate the time for them to dream, just as we allocate the time for them to study.

How many of the world's problems could we solve were we to pose the right questions to our children? Don't laugh. I assure you children could resolve issues that have perplexed generations, primarily because their young minds have not been tainted by the prejudice of the environment.

Practice visualizing your life the way you would like it to be. Unless you are content with ending up just anywhere, you had better have an idea where you are going. Be as precise as possibly when doing this exercise because the more detailed your vision becomes, the more powerful the impression it will make upon you.

Together, we will develop the map you need with the schematic outlined within these pages. Do not fret. Be patient. You are well on your way — whether you realize it or not. Remember, there is a systematic process that will provide the results you desire with the greatest consistency.

What Would Your Life Look Like?

What would your career, your marriage, and your relationships with your children, associates, and customers be like if your life were as you wanted it to be? How much time would you dedicate to your work, play, hobbies, and service to others? Avoid limiting yourself in any way; it is too soon to evaluate the feasibility of your dreams. If you are hesitant to follow my instruction, then perhaps you are still bound by limited thinking, thus denying yourself what you deserve. Open yourself to this concept: *anything* is possible. What do you have to lose? Get up to speed, and then continue.

Describe your dream home, vacation home, and the car you have been longing for. Describe your ideal companion and your desired weight, physical condition and habits. Should a negative voice within you ridicule the significance of such an exercise, you know what to do. There are little or no limitations;

you can become virtually anything to which you aspire. If you think you can or if you think you can't, you are right.

Please do not make light of this; it really works. When you want to achieve new and improved results, you have to do something different. This will work for you, just as it has for so many! Invest the time to envision your life as you would like it to be. Develop your own production titled, *The Life I Am Creating*. Do not critique yourself during the conceptualization process. Let your imagination soar freely amidst the possibilities.

"I never hit a shot, not even in practice, without having a very sharp, in-focus picture of it in my head." —Jack Nicklaus

Welcome back! Did you have some difficulty? If so, this is not unusual. After all, most of us have had little practice with this as adults. The practice may require some effort on your part. Keep it up and in time it will become easier.

Incidentally, what did you see, hear, smell, and taste? What were you doing, and how did it make you feel? The more detailed your vision is, the more readily your mind will accept it as though it were real. When you recognize your dreams are the precursor to creating your reality, you will do more of what is necessary to bring them to fruition. Do this repeatedly until your physical reality matches your vision, and remember the words of Hyrum Smith: "To reach any significant goal, you must leave your comfort zone."

What Gifts Do You Possess?

Regardless of who you are or what you have done, you have something to offer the world. You posses some distinguishing gifts you have likely suppressed as a result of your conditioning, or perhaps your gifts have atrophied because of your failure to recognize and exercise them. Each of us is born with a symphony within, awaiting the composer's realization of its existence.

Quit denying the voice beckoning you. You hear it play repeatedly. It calls you to rise and fulfill your life's purpose, but you have excused yourself, likely believing you do not have what it takes. You do! So what drives you to suppress your greatness? Do you fear your self-expression will result in the ridicule and rejection of your composition?

All of us have access to a universal river of knowledge and creativity—some have named this intuitiveness. Yet, most people fail to immerse themselves in the waters of this river and experience the introduction of their spiritual expression because they are overcome by fear.

Perhaps you will find yourself inspired by the story of Jay "Blue Jay" Greenberg, the twelve-year-old who some say is one of the greatest musical talents to come along in two hundred years. I was introduced to this remarkable young man while watching *60 Minutes* one Sunday evening. For the sake of accuracy I will quote verbatim a number of passages from the show.

"At twelve years of age, Jay has written five full-length symphonies, a feat that would take most a lifetime! He claims that the music fills his head and that he must write it down to get it out. Jay says he has no idea where the music comes from, but that it comes fully written—playing like an orchestra in his mind. When he composes, at times so rapidly that he often crashes his computer, it is as though he is downloading it from his mind. "We are talking about a prodigy of the level of the greatest prodigies in history when it comes to composition," says Sam Zyman, a composer. "I am talking about the likes of Mozart and Mendelssohn, and Saint-Sans."

Sam Zyman teaches music theory to Jay at the Julliard School in New York City, where he has taught for eighteen years. "This is an absolute fact. This is objective. This is not a subjective opinion," says Zyman. "Jay could be sitting here, and he could be composing right now. He could finish a piano sonata before our eyes in probably twenty-five minutes. And it would be a great piece."

According to Jay, "It's as if the unconscious mind is giving orders at the speed of light. You know, I mean, so I just hear it as if it were a smooth performance of a work that is already written, when it isn't."

Zyman says, "It's as if he's looking at a picture of the score, and he's just taking it from the picture, basically."

Jay's parents are as surprised as anyone. His father, Robert, is a linguist, and a scholar in Slavic language. His mother, Oma, is a painter who was born in Israel. Robert says Jay, who started writing and drawing instruments at age two, managed to draw and ask for a cello, even writing the word cello. Jay knew he wanted a cello, so his mother took him to a music store, where he was shown a miniature cello. He sat down and started playing it.

By the age of three, Jay was still drawing cellos, now as notes on a scale. Robert says, "He hears music in his head all the time, and he'll start composing, and he doesn't even realize it, probably, that he's doing it. But the teachers would get angry, and they would call us in for emergency meetings with seven people sitting there trying to figure out how they're going to accommodate our son." Jay's mother quotes Jay as saying, "I'm going to be dead if I am not composing. I have to compose. This is all that I want to do."

By the age of ten, Jay was attending Julliard, among the world's top conservatories of music, on a full scholarship. At age eleven, he was studying music theory with third-year college students.

Elizabeth Wolff is a concert pianist who works with Jay on his piano technique. "Jay writes things he can't even play, and he says he wants to perfect his piano playing, even though he doesn't need the piano."

Jay is fortunate, not only for the gift he possesses but also to have the support of his parents. Jay has in fact demanded his talent be recognized. Anything less would be cause for his demise. *Nothing less is acceptable.* His environment at home, school, and in life would have to adapt to accommodate his expression. Sure Jay is exceptional, but he is not alone. He is just one example of what can happen when society caters to the needs and the gifts of the individual. I can hear the critics whine, protesting the feasibility or manageability of such an undertaking: "It can't be done. We don't have the resources to provide the individual attention necessary for our children." Were all of us to think like this, the critics would be right! Contemplate what would happen were we to nurture the individual creativity of our children in great numbers. How might the world benefit? Do the possibilities justify the allocation of resources? Just look at the historical contributions made by a single individual. Multiply the potential a thousand-fold or a million-fold, and you may have an inkling of the possibilities.

Where do we begin? The best place is with us. You and I may not have been fortunate to have had parents who recognized our potential or who gave us encouragement and support. Regardless, we are likely privileged in some way or another. It is our responsibility, then, to identify our gifts and nurture them for ourselves. Like Jay, we will in turn be recognized for our unwavering commitment to create and contribute. We must be unwilling to settle for anything less.

In the same *60 Minutes* broadcast, I witnessed the irony within a segment featuring Dustin Hoffman, the actor, star, and icon of the film industry. Hoffman's acting career has spanned forty films in as many years. He states, "You cannot be in this," referring to his industry, "because you think you're going to make a living at it. You can only be in this. It's the only way you choose to survive." Note the parallel to Jay Greenberg's "I'm going to be dead if I am not composing." Hoffman later describes the motivation he derives when confronted with skepticism regarding his ability as an actor. "What fueled me then and what fuels me now is, 'Oh, you don't think I'm any good? You don't think I can do that.'" Hoffman compares acting to life: "Everything depends on a few decisions you make at the very beginning."

When questioned about his longtime friend, fellow actor Gene Hackman attributes Dustin Hoffman's success to his honesty, his unwillingness to compromise as an actor, and his willingness to take big chances. Hackman summed it up by saying, "He gets what he wants." This message resonates in the testimonial of one individual after another who has achieved success. Your determination, like theirs, must be uncompromising and unwavering. You must meet your obstacles with courage. Courage can best be defined as pressing forward in the presence of fear, doing something regardless of being terrified out of your mind at the prospect of doing it.

A few years back, I viewed a televised broadcast of Billy Joel addressing the faculty and student body of a Northeast university. Joel performed between questions and answers, offering viewers an opportunity to see him as they never had before. Numerous questions were posed to the artist. His response to one in particular will remain with me for life. Though I do not recall his words verbatim, I believe I grasped the greater message. In essence, Joel stated that to be successful in the arts you must eliminate all other options in your life. In other words, if you want to make it to the top in the entertainment industry, you cannot think about falling back on anything else. It does not work that way. Your dream isn't going to happen when you allow yourself an out. You must stand firm that absolutely nothing other than fulfilling your dream is an option. If you do not live your dream, you will die. So burn the ships behind you and live it! With respect to your dreams, you must not permit anything to divert your attention or adulterate your commitment. There cannot be a mistress awaiting you in the wings. You must remain faithful to your calling, uncompromised by the temptation of security, finding solace instead in your self-expression and creativity.

The Great Escape

As a personal coach, I have witnessed the misfortune of our readiness to compromise, to justify ourselves for doing so, and to conceal our despair. Instead of being honest, we choose to deceive ourselves, and those around us, into thinking we have accomplished what we desired to achieve. We then console ourselves with our vices and the company of others who will assure us that what we have done is right; however, we know better.

And so the multitudes consume their drugs, prescribed and otherwise. They drink their alcohol, indulge themselves with junk food, and tune in to mindless broadcasts while contemplating their next purchase. There is little to encourage us and much that leaves us questioning our condition. We cast blame on the establishment, conveniently forgetting that we are the establishment. All the while, deep down, they know they can do much better...but how dare someone propose they change. This is exactly what I am proposing! It is time we quit attempting to escape our present reality and instead create a new one.

Despite all I have described, these are still the best of times. I cannot imagine a time in history when people were better prepared to address what ails them. Knowledge is increasing faster than in any period of recorded history. Still, I find it perplexing when we make great strides in research and fail to implement what we have learned. For example, I have read university studies claiming that teenagers, to be functioning at peak performance, require at least nine hours of sleep. Parents of teenagers do not need a university study to confirm this; they already know. Teenagers typically have difficulty going to sleep before 12 a.m., and yet throughout much of the nation our school system requires that they rise by 6 a.m. to make class on time. What we get is a nation full of children who are half asleep through the better part of the day, and we wonder why so many are falling behind and failing to make the grade.

It gets even better! Medical research has demonstrated time and again how important it is for children to receive proper nutrition and exercise. Here's the reality: we feed our children junk food filled with empty calories but void of nutritional value. Deep-fried foods, fats, carbohydrates, and sugar dominate their daily lunch menu, not to mention the additives and preservatives. The food so many of our children eat is making them sick, hyperactive, and, in many instances, outright unmanageable. So what do we do? We put our children on medication. For the manufacturers of fast food and pharmaceuticals, it is a dream come true—a nation that willingly creates a new generation of addicts.

While we fatten our children to excess, we permit the same education system to eliminate recess and physical education programs that we are told have become cost prohibitive. This has been happening in school districts east to west, north to south—literally everywhere in our nation. So when are we going to care enough to do something about it? Even those who do not have children have a vested interest in the next generation. Children are the future of our nation. In fact, they are the future architects of our world. It is critical we understand children do not listen to what we say as much as they observe what we do!

Many examples in our society parallel what I have just addressed. We know something to be true and ignore it because we perceive it as inconvenient to act on. We must no longer compromise our children, our planet, or ourselves. I am sick and tired of the compromising—no more compromising for me! I am out to change things for the better, no matter how inconvenient it is. How about you? Are you with me? I hope so, for your sake and for the betterment of those you love. Discontentment with things as they are can often be the driving force behind the action required for change.

The True Measure of Our Success
"Set a goal to become a millionaire for what it makes of you to achieve it. Do it for the skills you have to learn and the person you have to become."
—Jim Rohn

We can foster a new understanding of what success is. We can share with our neighbors, our co-workers, and our families that success is not measured by one's income, possessions, social status, home, or car. Our *character*, rather, is the measure of our success, as are our contributions to others and the enjoyment derived from our daily lives.

The majority of us have been taught to compromise from childhood, and while we should consider the well-being of others at all times, we will experience far greater gratification when pursuing our life's passion without compromise. Ultimately, what is best for you is often best for those around you. Compromise is better placed aside with respect to pursuing your dreams, provided you truly desire to live them!

Begin here and now. There is no better time than the present. When you choose to pursue your dreams without succumbing to the negative influence of your environment, focusing on the joy of your craft and not the profit or pursuit of security, you will live in abundance. You will radiate with confidence and others will recognize it. People, opportunity, and prosperity will be drawn to you.

What Is Your Primary Objective?

Whatever you choose as your primary objective your thinking will play a critical role in your outcome, as will your behavior. A good start for adjusting your behavior is to begin by living within your means. You are not going to be very effective in accumulating wealth if you are consistently spending more than you are making. You may also consider furthering your education, thus increasing your value in the marketplace. A new job or career may be in order. Begin with your circumstances as they are.

As I have worked with individuals in financial matters over many years, I have discovered that the statistics are all too accurate. Most of us, regardless of income levels, stretch ourselves thin when spending. We make more, and then spend more, typically adjusting our lifestyles to the maximum and often beyond what our income will allow. We would be wise to observe those immigrating to America; they live modestly. Reducing our expenditures will permit us to save.

Presently, the average American household savings is at the lowest level since the Great Depression. The truth be known, we are spending more than we are making! In the coming pages we will take a closer look at some disturbing statistics.

Few among us cannot think of someone who has made, or has come into, a considerable sum of money, spending it as fast as they made it, ultimately finding themselves broke and deeply indebted. We also know those who earned modest incomes but disciplined themselves to live beneath their means, saving and investing to provide the independence they sought.

We are a nation of people seeking immediate gratification, demonstrating what little regard we truly have for freedom by imprisoning ourselves with the burden of debt. In contradiction to the principles of freedom to which our nation has aspired, millions are enslaved by our materialism. We succumb to the perception that what we own is synonymous with who we are. Attempting to compensate for our emptiness, we consume and surround ourselves with luxuries while giving little thought to the hardship it places upon our families, our spirit, and our environment. We work longer hours than the preceding generation for lesser pay so we can have the latest, the biggest, and the best — now.

Everyday millions of parents leave their children without supervision and guidance so they may work to purchase more. We live in a culture that spends vast sums of money on entertainment. Our nation's athletes not only earn millions to play, they also earn millions more to endorse overpriced shoes, apparel, etc. We purchase to appease the guilt for having sacrificed our children in pursuit of material things.

How Much Is Enough?

We may not recognize the error of our ways but we certainly feel it, witnessing it via the crime, drug addiction, and disrespect for others manifested by the new generation. Our nation and all that is truly valuable can be saved by re-evaluating our priorities and raising the bar of acceptable performance. As I stated earlier, we are so much better than what our present results would indicate.

You may be thinking that what I have shared thus far is all good and fine, but what you really desire to know is how to get what you want. It is pretty simple — you can begin by being grateful for what you already have! I started with little myself, and was at one time literally reduced to having nothing but the clothes on my back. The most difficult task I faced was in learning to become grateful for what it was I did have. Learning the value of patience was not easy for me either. I wanted everything *now*. I am not saying we shouldn't have a sense of urgency. Urgency is good when balanced with the confidence that the opportunity we seek will present itself at exactly the right time. Granted, this requires faith, and faith is usually born of experience. No matter how many times I emphasize the relevance of faith with respect to attaining your objectives, you are likely going to have to experience it for yourself.

How much is enough when it comes to income, possessions, wealth, and so forth? You are entitled to as much as it requires for you to fulfill your expectations or dreams. Life will give to you what you demand of it and seldom more! None of us are entitled to more than we can put to good use. We do a disservice to the world and to ourselves when we take more than we give. Though there are times we all take more than we should, we can strive to offset the imbalance of our consumption by focusing on and meeting the needs of others.

Union of Attitude and Behavior

Our dreams will not manifest themselves without us doing our part. A joint effort is required between you and the universe, and you will likely have to make some form of sacrifice to free yourself from a cycle of scarcity. For the most part, modern Americans have failed to recognize this. We insist on having the biggest and the best, as fast as possible, without regard to the consequences. This behavior is a manifestation of our scarcity mentality—if we don't get it now, we may never have the opportunity again. This type of thinking can create a great deal of hardship.

Managing Our Resources Better

Americans are exceptionally wealthy compared to the majority of the world's population, yet we are rather poor managers of the money we make. This can once again be attributed to the scarcity of our thinking and our attempt to supplement what is missing in our lives with material non-necessities.

"Lives based on having are less free than lives based on doing or being."
—E. Y. Harburg

"It's not what you gather, but what you scatter that tells the kind of life you have lived."
—Helen Walton

I have witnessed the impact of the American consumer mentality in my own life as well as in the lives of others. I am a strong supporter of productivity and progress. I am just questioning whether we are sacrificing the things that are truly important for the material goods we don't really need. Have you compromised your relationships, your freedom, and your happiness in exchange for something else, only to realize how desperately screwed up your priorities were? Don't beat yourself up; just recognize what you have been missing out on and turn it around. The book *Affluenza*, by John De Graaf, David Wann, and Thomas H. Naylor, may be a great tool in helping you to put your consumer behavior in perspective and more importantly take control of your financial affairs.

Affluenza sounds like a disease, doesn't it? Indeed, the premise of this book is that the American consumer culture can be likened to a diseased state, subverting the quality of life. I've cautioned my children for years that what we own owns us. Unfortunately, I learned it the hard way. After having read *Affluenza,* I truly started evaluating the true cost of what I considered purchasing, and I found myself hesitant to allow a possession to own me.

You likely recall the exercise in the first session when we discussed our priorities—how everything comes into perspective for us when we are faced with imminent death. You undoubtedly indicated your families and your relationships are of the utmost importance to you. But when was the last time you took a vacation with the people you love? For those of you who say you can't make the time or don't have the money, remember that if you think you can or you think you can't, you're right.

Take a good look around you and identify someone you know who is a self-made success—the type of success that permits the individual to do whatever they want to do, where and when they choose to do it. Does this person make excuses? Do they readily accept that something cannot be done? Do they understand the word *no?* What in heaven's name is preventing you from doing what you so desperately want to do? Seriously, what is the problem? The first step is in identifying what is restricting you and then finding a way to go around it, crawl under it, knock it down, and trample over it. Or better yet, come to the realization that *it* never really was holding you back. The truth is, *you* are holding yourself back, and all you have to do is recognize this. Now put as much energy and determination into getting where you want to be. It is so much easier when you get out of your own way.

Most of us are not where we would like to be because we have failed to identify what we desire to accomplish in the first place. Or we don't have the foggiest idea of how we can get there, agreed? So what we have to do is seek out someone who has been where we want to go. Many great resources are available to will facilitate your advancement. Robert T. Kiyosaki's *Rich Dad, Poor Dad* provides a foundation of practical principles for effectively building and managing wealth. Kiyosaki tells of the two men who influenced him most in his childhood — one who conformed to the more traditional role prescribed by society, and the other, who took the road less traveled. This book will undoubtedly enlighten many of you to the possibilities that exist for every individual who possesses the determination to gain true financial independence. Place it on your required reading list if you have not already read it.

To become wealthy, we must think and act as the wealthy do. The problem is, most of us do not perceive the lifestyles of the wealthy accurately. We envision yachts, jets, mansions, and exotic vacations as the norm, when it is not necessarily the reality. The *Millionaire Next Door*, by Thomas J. Stanley and William D. Danko, exposes the inaccuracy of the American paradigm — what it is to be rich, how the so-called "other half" lives, what their behavioral patterns and purchasing practices are, and much more. If you have not read it already, this book is also a must.

Many people fail to achieve prosperity and independence because they have a false understanding of what is required to obtain them. Most of the people described as self-made millionaires made considerable sacrifices early on. They refused to pursue instant gratification. They understood that wealth is not built by paying astronomical interest rates on the acquisition of consumer goods, investing instead in education, formal and informal.

What could you go without for a while? Eliminate something from your lifestyle that would permit you to place some money each month into a savings account. You must make your money work for you or you will always be working for your money. To implement a successful savings strategy, you will have to pay yourself first. When you pay others before yourself, there will seldom be anything remaining for you. The only way to change your results is to change your practices.

Some of you might be saying, "Hey, hold on a minute Mark. I thought you said this book was about getting what I want and living my dreams, but you're laying all of this work on me." I did, and I am. We must align ourselves with the elements that promote health, wealth, freedom, and happiness. Only then will they materialize in our lives. Rest assured you will not come by, let alone retain, any of these for long without making some form of sacrifice.

Take an accounting of what you are spending each month. Reference your checkbook and your receipts for the past three months, categorizing your expenditures: mortgage or rent, utilities, groceries, automotive, fuel, clothing, food, and so forth. Calculate the monthly average. Could you give up that daily cappuccino? Look at the numbers. At $3.50, one cappuccino daily multiplied by twenty-two working days each month equals $77 every month. That's $924 each year. Now identify something additional you can make a daily, weekly, or monthly reduction in; it all adds up faster than you think. Remember the story of Mr. Huang, who made the "Forbes Four Hundred"? He started his business with the $13,000 he and his wife saved and consequently turned his original investment into a financial empire. What will you do with your savings?

In this session, we discussed a number of things that will promote your financial independence. At minimum, you recognize the importance of learning from and mirroring the performance of the masters. Whatever you seek, understand the value of combining a positive attitude with constructive behavior. As we close this session remember to practice your visual exercises frequently: see yourself living in abundance every day. Additionally, review the session summary and complete your exercises for the week. I look forward to our next session together.

Session 4 Summary

- You are in good company when you permit yourself to dream.
- Visualize your life the way you would like it to be.
- Every human being is born with a symphony within.
- Identify your gift.
- Do not settle for anything less than you deserve.
- Our character is the true measure of our success.
- Reprioritize.
- Your attitude is everything.
- Emulate the masters.

Your Exercises for the Week

1. Visualize your life the way you would like it to be, and do so often.
2. Make a list of your gifts. What comes naturally to you?
3. Review your present expenditures and identify those you can reduce or eliminate from your budget.
4. Implement a savings and investment plan. Consider starting a business, even if it is part time to begin with.
5. Review your priorities and identify the masters in the areas you wish to improve in.

Session Review

COMMIT YOURSELF

"The moment you commit and quit holding back, all sorts of unforeseen incidents, meetings, and material assistance will rise up to help you. The simple act of commitment is a powerful magnet for help." —Napoleon Hill

Welcome to Session Five with your personal coach. By now you should be recognizing some improvement in the areas of your life you have been focusing on. Do not worry if the results are not coming as fast as you had hoped. Your dreams will unfold in good time. In this session I will reveal the significant power we possess when we are truly committed.

What Are You Committed to Accomplishing?

We touched lightly on commitment in the previous session. Now we will take a closer look at the important role your commitment and accountability play in achieving your success.

Accountability promotes the strength of your commitment. The act of commitment is tempered like steel when we announce our absolute resolve to complete an undertaking, all the while refusing to yield to the pessimistic opinions of our critics. Like Dustin Hoffman, tell me I cannot do something and I will prove you wrong. We must access the power possessed in our fortitude, holding steadfast to what we have determined in our competent judgment to be right. We can adjust our course when new information suggests it would be in our best interest to do so.

Be cautious when selecting individuals to share your dreams with. Confide in those who have achieved favorable results themselves. Turn to the joyful friend who will encourage you and offer you support. Do not waste your time or dispel your optimism by sharing your ambitions with the pessimist; they will deplete your energy. Though such individuals will never admit to their own depravity, they will be happy to sit with you for hours and discuss the imperfections of others. Disassociate yourself from their like as fast as you can.

You need not abandon a loved one who struggles with a negative self-image, or from a negative outlook in general. Merely evaluate your ability or inability to function at peak performance while exposed to a continuous flow of negativity from any source. Should you determine the source of negativity undermining your self-confidence, faith, and progress is directly attributed to someone with whom you have strong emotional ties, you may need to confront that person and alert them to the discomfort they cause. Perhaps you have already attempted this and have only found yourself further depleted of your vital optimism and energy. Should this be the case, encourage the person to seek help outside of your relationship. This may pose a substantially greater risk than simply stepping back from the relationship and taking greater precautions in what you choose to share. Should you still remain dependent on your negative relationship after having made the effort, it would serve you to consider who is truly responsible for the negative environment.

Think of someone you highly respect. This individual is probably a qualified candidate with whom you can share your dreams and to whom you can proclaim your intentions. Should your trusted friend respond unfavorably, you are not bound by their judgment, only wise to consider their perspective! Make a decision and then ask the individual to hold you accountable to the decision you have made. When you commit to someone whom you truly respect, your constructive ego, as I refer to it, becomes attached to the outcome. This driving force may be the result of your desire to save face or to prove you are capable of accomplishing the very thing you declared you would. You may be forced to concede that you alone do not possess all the knowledge, tools, and alliances required to complete the task at hand. You will discover they lie dormant, only to be awakened at your beckoning.

I Am Who I Am

The power of "I am" is misunderstood and misused by the majority. Don't deceive yourself. The "I am" is a major contributor to how we project ourselves, what we accomplish, and who we become. For example, "I am so fat," "I am not feeling well," "I am broke," "I am miserable," "I am lonely," and so forth. In stating the "I am," we invoke a power far greater than our understanding. When misused, that power can lead us to the very plight of which we find ourselves complaining. When used properly, that power gives us great potential.

Are you using your "I am" carefully? You will benefit immensely by demonstrating caution in how you introduce your declarations to the universe. The following are some examples of how the "I am" should be constructively used: "I am becoming thinner every day," "I am feeling great today," "I am in a temporary cash-flow crisis and am implementing measures to correct it." You may have chuckled when you read this, but it really works. If you are a student of human development, you recognize the process of using affirmations. This by no means even begins to accurately describe the power of the "I am." When proclaiming the source of his authority, Christ said, "I am the way, the truth, and the life; no one goes to the Father except by me." [1]

What title do you claim for yourself? How would you describe your identity? For the moment, see yourself as a completed work, not a work in progress. What do you look like and who have you become? Ask yourself what you may have done to become as successful as you are. Let your imagination run wild; don't worry, you are not likely to become carried away with yourself. You will most likely find that your perceptions are going to require some considerable effort and time to reconstruct.

---

[1] **John 14:6,** <u>Good News Bible</u>, the American Bible Society, New York, 1966.

Quality Questions, Quality Answers

Few things are more important to us in creating the life we desire than learning how to ask quality questions. Greater wisdom is found within the questions you ask of yourself and of the world around you, than within the answers you seek.

It has been said ours is not to question why. The fact is *why* can often be a poor question. "Why me?" we ask when faced with an undesired circumstance. Questions such as, "Why do things like this always seem to happen to me?" are sure to trigger a negative response from the subconscious mind. Our subconscious must respond, so be sure to consider the quality of the question posed along with its predisposition to render a negative response. Your mind will not lie dormant when presented with a question as direct as this. It will respond; it must. Asking *why me* typically provides us little more than an overwhelming sense of futility. When you pose a question that implies you are a victim, you will remain a victim.

"The one thing your brain can't do is NOT try to find the answer to the question that is presented to it; that is, once you ask the human brain—yourself, the universe—a question, you can't NOT try to find the answer to it."
—Noah St. John

I incorporated Lifeworks International in August of 1997 for the purpose of advancing progressive thinking in life and business. The catchphrase of our company is, "You'll find that LIFEWORKS when you ask the right questions." I have long understood the power contained within the questions we ask. Every profession is subject to learning and asking the proper questions to facilitate the introduction of appropriate solutions. In the sales process, questions are critical when assessing the needs and desires of a prospective customer. At the onset of my career, I heard this referred to as *fact finding*, as impersonal as it may sound. Years later many of us would become familiar with Stephen Covey's advice: "Seek first to understand, then to be understood" — a more contemporary way to define an age-old practice of unveiling the needs and desires of those we come into contact with. I refer to this as "Discovery and Recommendation."

As I stated at the onset of this book, life's critical elements that provide for success have been present since the creation of life itself. We can interpret them, build on them, and repackage them so they may continue to find their way into the lives of others just as they have found their way into ours. All great innovations have been created at the hands of those who dared to pose great questions.

What Questions Have You Been Asking?

How could you improve upon the questions you have been asking? Do the questions you have been asking posture your mind defensively, or do they create a co-operative alliance with the solution-oriented resources of your mind? Review this example: Are you inclined to ponder your fate, as we previously addressed with questions like, "Why am I always the one who gets @#$% on?" Or, "Why does this @#$% always happen to me?" Or do you ask yourself solution-based questions like, "What can I do to improve?" Or, "How can I resolve whatever I need to resolve?" Or, "Where does the solution to my problem lie?" Questions like these require a constructive response from your mind, and your mind cannot help but search out an answer. Take a moment and examine the questions you have been asking yourself and the way in which your mind has been responding.

Some of you may be thinking you have searched long and hard for the answers, exhausting every reasonable option, to no avail. To this I respond with a quote by Thomas Edison..."**You have tried only reasonable things. Reasonable things never work. Thank God you can't think up any more reasonable things, so you'll have to begin thinking up unreasonable things to try, and now you'll hit the solution in no time.**"

Society would often have you suppress anything remotely resembling the unorthodox or unreasonable. Instead, it would have you conform and remain safely sheltered within its embrace. At times, the embrace constricts so tightly it literally squeezes the life from the adventurous spirit. Do not let this happen to you.

A World of Possibilities

What would this world look like were we to double, triple, or quadruple the numbers among us who break free from conformity? What would we achieve were we to actually believe humanity could live in peace and that anything less was absolutely, unconditionally unacceptable? Would we eliminate hunger throughout the world were we to simply accept it is feasible for us to do so? Would we eradicate disease entirely were we to eliminate the financial gain in perpetuating it?

Questions such as these have been asked before, and it is up to you and me to continue asking them. We must ask questions of those who govern us. We must ask *how* we can accomplish these things and more. We have to demand the leadership of individuals who will find a way. There must be those among us who possess the vision—leaders who can gain the cooperation of other leaders and thus inspire all nations, religions, races, and cultures to unite in such an undertaking.

Though such challenges as war, hunger, poverty, and abuse of the Earth's ecosystem appear to be the more colossal of the obstacles humanity faces, they pale in comparison to our fear. It is our fear that constrains us—the fear that we may become, or we already are, vulnerable. We fear we will somehow lose something more precious than peace—abundance and self-expression. We fear we might lose our souls if we were to acknowledge that we are responsible for all that ails us. For how dare we be so bold as to claim that we are great enough to deliver ourselves from our sins! We ignore our free will, declaring that we are victims of those who have lived before us. We must not continue to prescribe to a doctrine shrouded in the name of religion, rendering our will useless. When we hear another speak from scarcity, we must speak from abundance.

There are those who prosper in war, in hunger, and in illness. Take away the prosperity in such things and attach it instead to the task of creating a better world! Don't we all desire a better world in which to live? As you demand a better life for yourself, you also demand a new and better reality for our world. When enough people insist, the change will begin. What number will be needed? It is difficult to say, but it will require great leadership. The obstacles may appear insurmountable, yet it can be done. It is not *if*, but *how* and *when*. Step forward and lead, for your sake, the sake of the children, and the sake of the human race. Begin at home and in your community. Be a better person — make a difference. The world needs you!

"Never let the fear of striking out get in your way."
— Babe Ruth

Step Up to the Plate and Swing

Implement the power of the "I am" in pronouncing who you are and what your intent is. The "I am" is the declaration of your commitment, and it brings about miracles in life. You may question how you can commit without understanding at the onset all the fulfilling your commitment will entail. Should this still be the case, I ask you to once again reference the words of Napoleon Hill at the beginning of this session. You do not need to have all the answers or possess all the skills required to accomplish your objective when you first commit. It is far more important you have a clear picture of the end result you desire. There is a way to accomplish almost anything, and it will be revealed through your persistent efforts.

Have faith. Everything you will require to complete what you have started will find its way to you. The power within the act of faith is unsurpassed, perhaps unmatched. *To have faith is to acknowledge the existence of something greater than you, and in this acknowledgment lays your ability to witness miracles.* Through this acknowledgment you become aligned, working cooperatively and synergistically with the universe. When you commit, introductions will be made, opportunities will be presented, and solutions will prevail.

Session 5 Summary

- Commit yourself.
- Be cautious with whom you share your dreams.
- Make yourself accountable.
- Implement the power of "I am."
- Observe the questions you are asking.
- Think of the unreasonable things you can do.
- Examine yourself for faulty perceptions.
- Beware: fear constrains us more than anything.

Your Exercises for the Week

1. Review the commitments you have made to date. Have you been holding anything back? Write down your new commitments, and share them with a trusted friend or family member.

2. Reflect on and make note of the "I am" declarations you use daily. What power are you invoking?

3. What questions are you asking? Do they render a negative or positive response? Write a list of the negative questions you have been asking and then rewrite them so they yield positive or constructive responses.

4. Look to the unreasonable for new solutions to old problems. Make note of your ideas. Trusting this to memory is not recommended. Write down ideas as they come to you.

Session Review

_____
_____
_____
_____
_____
_____
_____
_____
_____
_____
_____
_____
_____
_____
_____
_____

SESSION 6
PRIORITIZE

Welcome to Session Six with your personal coach. Those who find themselves this far along with our sessions have surely made the commitment to finish the entire series. There is much awaiting you!

The Dullest Pencil Is Greater Than the Sharpest Mind

Many management courses emphasize the importance of writing notes to yourself as ideas come to you, or as you are presented with information you may need to recall at some future date. This is good advice and certainly worth re-emphasizing, particularly because the majority of us still fail to follow it with any consistency. Brilliant insights can be fleeting. Keep a notepad, tape recorder, or daily planner close by in case you feel inspired.

As you progress through your day, you will undoubtedly face interruptions distracting you. Add even the smallest tasks to your to-do list, and make a note of the time devoted to them. As you complete each task remember to cross them off. You will discover how good it feels to witness your increased productivity, and this will empower you throughout the day and throughout your project. The most successful executive will increase their productivity, as well as the productivity of their employees, by recording their activities and the resulting progress.

This process is not only an effective way to measure progress; it is also a great way to track how efficient you are with respect to managing your time.

Are You Prioritizing Effectively?

As you add to your list, prioritize the urgency of each task. A good way to establish your prioritization process is to implement the ABC method: "A" being a top priority, or one providing you with the greatest return for the time invested; "B" representing a lesser priority but one still deserving your attention; "C" signifying a task that may be delegated to another, thus permitting you to focus on "A" and "B". Remember, time is finite; utilize this precious commodity wisely.

Yes, Maybe, No, and Never.

When we say "yes" or commit ourselves to anything or anyone, we must likely say "no" to another opportunity. Be cautious when committing yourself. Doing so means you will be unavailable if a more profitable or favorable opportunity arises. When you do commit, do your best to keep your commitment, despite whatever discomfort you may experience in so doing.

In keeping your commitments, you will gain the trust of others, distinguishing yourself from the competition. Your good reputation will lead to new opportunities and garner the support you will likely need to achieve your goals. Exceptional, true leaders keep their commitments. As for the word *maybe*, it's a favored way to sidestep committing to anything. Stop using it, particularly with your children.

Delegating Is Duplicating

Many executives and business owners fail to plan, prioritize, and delegate as routinely as they should. This can be attributed to their failure to recognize the substantial benefit the process provides. They may also fear the work may not be completed in a timely manner or to the level of their expectations. Such individuals prescribe to the old adage, "If you want something done right, do it yourself." This is a mistake when it comes to "B" and "C" tasks. Delegate as often as your circumstances will permit, and always follow up when you have delegated a task to another. For those of you, who desire to become masters of your life, learn to master managing people. The cooperative effort of those around you is the gateway to your success.

Making Money with Support from Others

Money is far from the most important thing in our lives. Sure, it can make things easier, but it is not nearly as important as the overall quality of life. I would give up everything I have accumulated in exchange for my health or the health of a loved one. Wouldn't you? I am not downplaying the value of money and all the comfort and conveniences it brings. I hope you feel good about making all the money you desire. I want you to feel good about it. You should feel good about it. The better you feel about having money, the more likely you are to attract it. I also hope you will be generous with your money. Giving generously is tantamount to living in abundance. Givers gain.

People come to my workshops with the primary intent to learn how to significantly increase their incomes because people believe money will provide security, freedom, and material goods. Most everyone would lead you to believe they want more money. It is surprising, however, how many people feel guilty about it!

My workshops are designed to provide skills that facilitate financial success; however, this is the least of what they offer. More importantly, they focus on creating abundance in all areas of life. The more we focus on becoming a better person, the more readily our needs and desires are met. Money is the byproduct of providing quality service to others. Focus on what you can do to assist others and the money will come! Offer others the opportunity to work, and you will make even more money.

Let us take a closer look at how important delegation can be in your life and your business with respect to money and the freedom it provides. For an individual who makes thirty, fifty, or one hundred dollars per hour to spend his time completing a task that could easily be completed by another who commands only ten dollars per hour would be foolish. Many of us simply refuse to give up control, and this is why our lives are often out of control. An executive would not dream of hiring an individual at a hundred dollars per hour to fill a position warranting a fraction of that amount. It just does not happen. Nevertheless, many executives will spend their own time completing such tasks rather than outsourcing them.

Taking time to reassess your priorities can do wonders for your income and your relationships. Remember, when you can delegate, delegate! There is a good chance you can delegate more frequently than you think. Think about why you may be hesitating to delegate the simplest of tasks in your business and personal life. Whatever the reason, work it out and get over it. Your time is far too valuable to both you and those who desire to spend more time with you.

Procrastination Is Costly

When we do not want to do something, regardless of its importance, we are remarkably proficient at procrastinating. A great way to move beyond procrastinating is to re-associate your pain-pleasure response to the activity you find yourself avoiding.

A good example of how I accomplished this involves a sales professional who was dealing with some confidence issues. He avoided activities placing him in front of prospective customers—not a good thing for someone dependent on sales for a living. Most people liked this man because he was the type to just go with the flow; however, he seized every opportunity to find or create busy work excusing him from his true purpose, which was to seek out prospective customers. You will not be surprised to learn he wasn't making his quota. "I just don't have enough time," he would say. Determining this was not the case after analyzing his daily activities, calls, and follow-ups, I immediately moved to address the real problem.

People usually avoid what they feel uncomfortable doing. We are typically uncomfortable with the unknown and with things that make us feel inadequate. Appropriate education, training, and experience usually put those in sales at ease. They become comfortable, and most importantly, they become confident when approaching others with the intent of serving them. It really comes down to identifying the source of resistance. In most cases it is because they do not believe in themselves or in the value of their product or service.

Understanding their deficiency is half the battle. The rest of the battle can be addressed by assessing the value of what one has to offer and believing it will benefit a reasonable percentage of those who buy it. Qualifying the needs and desires of the prospect are critical in establishing whether there is a measurable value that justifies moving forward with the transaction. With respect to this particular salesman, the key lied in moving him to recognize the value of what he had to offer. Once he accepted this, his *pain* subsided.

We fail to progress because our perceptions are faulty and lead us to a great deal of pain. To avoid pain, we avoid whatever it is we should be doing. Ironically, this behavior leads to the pain of not being productive, compounding feelings of inadequacy, and the pain of failing to provide for those who depend on us. The only way to break free of this is to change the way we perceive something. The way to do this is to introduce new information. When someone has made up their mind about something, it is difficult to change that persons mind unless new and valid information is introduced to justify it.

With respect to this salesman, he did not want to call on prospects for fear of interrupting them. He did not want to be rude or pushy. He, like the majority of us, hated pushy salespeople, and he was not about to be counted among them. Above all he did not want to be rejected.

When he began to recognize what he had to offer was truly of considerable value, and though some might initially be hesitant to meet with him, the majority was often won over by his confidence, sincerity, and the value they perceived. All he had to do was get right down to it and the pain of the unknown became overshadowed by the pain of being without. In a brief period of time his confidence grew, one success led to another, and the task he once dreaded became something he looked forward to. I witnessed a complete turnabout in his outlook and performance—all because he recognized the value he offered. And you know what? Once he recognized it, so did his prospective customers.

Do you want to quit procrastinating? Then recognize your value to the world. If you do not think you have anything to offer, think again. Some work may be required on your part to prepare and position yourself but it's worth working for. You owe it to yourself, and you owe it to the rest of us. So if you have not done so already, pull out a pen and paper and prepare to write your to-do list at the completion of this session.

Attention to Time Yields Big Returns

A great time to contemplate the things on your to-do list for the coming day is the evening before. Dedicate a few minutes when you are likely to be uninterrupted and assess your priorities. What must you accomplish in the coming day? Indicate the level of priority, remembering your ABC's. Do this religiously every night for the next ninety days, and it will become habitual for you.

What Constitutes an "A" Priority?

At the top of my "A" priority list is my children. For example, I have listed my children's sports games, music recital, birthdays, and events recognizing their athletic and academic achievements as "A" priorities. These things are so important to me that without a doubt they became the leading motivator behind developing my own company, thus assuring control of my schedule. The thought of missing their elementary school parades, their games, and their concerts disturbed me. As my children's childhoods fade into memories, I can tell you I have no regrets about having witnessed their special moments. Not one possession can compare to the time in their company.

You may not currently be in a position to spend the time you would like with your family. If this is the case, seek out a way to permit you to do so. Make it a priority. There is no second chance to recapture childhood moments. Unfortunately, many people compromise what really matters most, only to regret it later. Of course, we all must make a living, which requires sacrifice. Just be cautious that you are not using work as an excuse. Be careful with what you are sacrificing. Early in our relationship, my wife and I decided she would stay home to raise the children. We did without many of the material things our friends took for granted, but the rewards have been numerous. I would do the same thing again, only I would not give it a second thought as I did then.

The purpose of our sacrifice became apparent as our children grew. They are fine people. My wife and I clearly understand the blessings of having provided them the attention they deserved. Every game, every concert, and every function we attended had a purpose. Our participation echoed our affection more loudly than the words "I love you" ever could. We told them we loved them as well—numerous times every day—but nothing speaks as clearly as action, and nothing resonates like commitment. The homes, the cars, the toys, and all the trappings came in good time. Though my wife and I have been blessed materially, it is still and always will be the relationships with our children we value most.

When Do You Feel Best about Yourself?

I find I am happiest when I am in a creative state, implementing and living in accordance with the principles of abundance. People are constantly creating. As I emphasize to my children, if we are not creating something constructive, you can be assured we are creating something destructive. We are creators! What have you been creating, and does it meet your expectations? If not, you can begin anew. It does not matter who you are or what you may have done, you can reinvent yourself!

You deserve to discover what is truly important to you and what will provide for your happiness. Understanding what really makes you happy will draw you closer to the results you desire. How can we begin to prioritize when we fail to define what it is we want in the first place? Most people do not have a clear understanding of what they want. When asked what they want, they respond with, "I don't know, but it would be nice to have a lot of money." Their lives are frequently as mundane as their response. Those who achieve any significant level of success are typically quite clear about what they want. These people are decisive, confident, and far more likely to trust their own judgment.

Trust your judgment or you will hesitate; you must have a plan or you will flounder. Do not be afraid of making mistakes, and do not worry if your plan is rudimentary at first. Your mistakes will bring you around to the right path in time. You will likely experience your share of discomfort and some painful consequences along the way, but you will become a better person for having experienced them.

Write out your list of things to do. Call it your Life List—things you absolutely have to do before you die. Give your attention to the smallest details. Realize this is a critical step to achieving your dreams!

Session 6 Summary

- Increase your effectiveness by prioritizing.
- Be careful what you commit to, and keep your commitments.
- Delegating is duplicating.
- A little time invested in planning yields big returns.

Your Exercises for the Week

1. Complete your Life's List of things to do—things you absolutely have to do before you die.
2. Review your to-do list for the coming week.
3. Assign a priority "A," "B," or "C" to each task. Further prioritize each task: 1 to indicate the highest priority, 2 the next, and so on.
4. Assess the commitments you have made, and determine how well you have followed through. What costs have you paid for failing to keep your word?
5. What tasks can you delegate? Who will you delegate them to? Create a list of tasks, and assign them to the individuals you have identified.
6. Begin planning each evening for the coming day. Prioritize your list of things to do, and break down complex tasks into smaller activities.

Session Review

SESSION 7
PLAN TO SUCCEED

Welcome to Session Seven with your personal coach.

Everything Has Its Price

We have all heard it said that everything has a price connected to it. There is a price to pay if you want to make things better; a price to pay for leaving things just as they are; a price for everything. Many choose to remain as they are because they associate more pain with the effort required to change. Perhaps they are afraid things could be worse were they to do something different, and the unknown terrifies them. So they choose to play it safe, or so they think. They associate more pain with the possibility of failure than remaining in their present discomfort and despair. As they observe those who risk and succeed, they proclaim that their good fortune can be attributed to luck.

Remember the significance of the two greatest motivators of human beings—pain and pleasure. Success can be attributed to understanding the role they play in the decision-making process. Remember, pain appears to play the predominant role of the two, and when focused constructively, it can catapult the most complacent into action. *When the pain we associate with remaining as we are is greater than the pain we associate with change, we will change.*

It is safe to assume you know how to implement significant change in you life, or you would not have progressed this far with our sessions. I am not out to drive this point into the ground, though I must drive it home. Understanding the motivational power of pain and pleasure, and implementing them accordingly can make all the difference in your life. If you have not already discovered this, you soon will.

Initiating Your Plan

"Decide what you want. Then write it all down. Put a lot of little things on there so you can start checking some things off, because part of the fun of having the list is checking it off." —Jim Rohn

One of life's greatest joys is the process of simply beginning. So where do you begin? It is not as difficult as we often think. Start by writing down your ideas. Refrain from judging their feasibility. Simply write what comes to you. For the time being, avoid using the term *goals*. Just write a list of things to do today, this week, this month, throughout the year, and over your lifetime. Give attention to the every detail; the greater the detail, the more vivid your mental picture will become. As your visualization gains clarity, it begins to form a new reality for you. This is very important. When you become proficient at visualizing your dreams, you will discover that life is a canvas, and you can create the life you desire at will. There is much work to be done, but you have begun. You will recall the old adage, "A journey of a thousand miles begins with a single step."

A Picture Is Worth a Thousand Words

As you think you will write and as you write you will think. We think in pictures, and we convert our language into visual images within our minds. I remember one Sunday afternoon a number of years ago, my wife requested I take the children out to play while she prepared dinner—a gracious way of informing me she needed some time to herself. So my three oldest children and I set off on a bike ride through the neighborhood, while Tresha and our infant son remained at home.

Normally, the children were restricted to riding on our street, the distance of a few houses in either direction. Considering they were under my direct supervision, I extended the boundary several blocks to the neighborhood park, where there was ample space for them to ride and play. In doing this, we crossed a major intersection with posted speeds of forty miles per hour. We crossed safely and arrived at the park where the children's attention diverted to the jungle gym. There we played our favorite game, freeze tag, until I laughed and ran myself to exhaustion. To this day I do not know who had more fun, the children or me.

There we were on this summer day, having the time of our lives without a care in the world. It was one of those moments we wish would last forever. The day quickly slipped away as it does when you are having fun, and I realized my wife was expecting us to return any moment. To the children's disappointment, I informed them it was time to make our way home. So we were off on our bikes, when once again we approached the busy intersection. This time the light was red. We stood on the sidewalk along the street's edge, the children by my side. I was careful to make sure they waited for the light to turn green and the traffic to clear. The words I used remain forever imprinted in my mind.

"Don't step into the street."

Before I could blink, one of my sons had stepped forward directly into the path of a fast-moving red compact pickup. To this day, I am not sure how I was able to reach him as quickly as I did. To our good fortune, I grabbed his shoulder, pulling him, bike and all, clear of the pickup. Had I hesitated for an instant, I am sure he would not be with us today. My heart racing and pounding, I calmly inquired at the top of my lungs, "Didn't you hear me?"

"You told us to go daddy!" he exclaimed.

"No I didn't, son. I told you *not* to step into the street; you need to listen to your father!" I responded. The event replayed in my mind throughout the remainder of the day, and finally it dawned on me that my son was right.

To preface what I will be sharing with you momentarily, I draw your attention to the incident and the way I have just described it to you. I am confident you will acknowledge as you read the story that you actually visualized much, if not all, of what I described. You saw the children, their bikes, the park, the jungle gym, the busy intersection, the compact pickup, and so forth. At some point you may have even experienced the acceleration of your own heart rate and a heightened level of anxiety. The level of emotional participation can obviously vary. Nevertheless, you saw the story play out in your mind.

You translated my language into visual images, just as my son did. I said to the children, "Don't step into the street." What is the visual message in this instruction? It is the act of stepping into the street. The visual message conflicted with my intent to have my children remain safely on the sidewalk. My son's body followed his mind — an instant response to my instruction as he visually interpreted it.

It is a blessing my other children processed my instruction differently, or perhaps they were delayed in their response. Though I cannot be certain as to why they did not follow their brother's lead, I can state that my other children are highly analytical; their brother, however, is expressive. I believe this had everything to do with the way they responded to my instruction. The expressive personality tends to respond quickly to information and act accordingly. The analytical personality thinks things through and is typically more deliberate in their actions. We will discuss predominant personality traits in session 10. For now, we will focus on what I refer to as pictorial communication, or pictorial processing.

We think in pictures, and we would be well served to understand the relevance of this human trait. We frequently introduce our ideas or instructions to others with language structured in such a way as to create the opposite pictorial image of what we intended to convey. Do you remember the original anti-drug campaign of the early 1980s: "Don't do drugs"? You may not be old enough to recall this, yet you likely recognize the conflicting message nonetheless. "Don't do drugs" creates a visualization of witnessing or participating in the very act of using drugs. Fortunately, the campaign was revised. The slogan as it stands today, "Just say no," does not even bring drugs into the message. "Just say no" creates a visual image of empowerment. Our children see an individual, likely themselves, standing firm, confident in the decision to do what is right!

I recall a billboard I passed numerous times in the Salt Lake City metropolitan area. The billboard displayed the photograph of a young muscular man wearing what was obviously a nurse's uniform—the caption beneath read, "Nursing isn't for wimps," or something to that effect. Obviously the intent was to dispel the notion that nursing is a profession for women alone. Truth be known, nursing was at one time dominated by males. What bothered me was the use of conflicting messages. Wouldn't it be more effective to be consistent by showing an image of the muscular young man and a caption that read, "Nursing is for the strong"?

I have great respect for nursing, which is why I called the number listed on the billboard. A recorded message asked callers to leave their information so someone could get back to them. I gave my name, number, and a brief explanation as to why I was calling. Then I offered some constructive advice I believed would enhance the recruiting success of this organization.

Approximately a year later I encountered the man responsible for designing the nursing campaign; he was one of many who responded to a recruiting ad for one of my companies. When I learned of his background I informed him I was the individual who had called some months ago. I asked if he had any recollection of my call. He did, and we laughed.
We then discussed the relative success he had experienced with the billboard. I still ponder whether he would have been seeking new employment had this particular recruiting campaign been more effective.

The identical mental process you use to convert words into visual images will serve you in the visualization and planning process. When initiating your plan, there is no need to be concerned with whether you have all the answers, resources, and capital required to accomplish your objective at the onset. You would not be as quickly discouraged were you to focus as much on the possibilities as you are inclined to focus on the obstacles. You may think you are simply being realistic; you would be better off being a bit more unreasonable. By approaching your objective as cautiously as you are, you are probably imposing more limitations upon yourself than truly exist. This concept may meet some resistance with respect to your present thinking. Get over it and focus on the end result you desire instead of on all the things you think are standing in your way. If you are like the majority, you have been focusing on your limitations for far too long. Where has this gotten you?

No One Has All the Answers

When John F. Kennedy announced his intent to place a man on the moon, do you think he encountered resistance? You bet he did! Do you think for one moment Kennedy and the scientific community of his day had all the answers as to how this could be accomplished? Absolutely not! The fact is they were far from possessing many of the answers necessary to accomplish this remarkable feat. Regardless, the scientific community moved forward with a clear image of the goal in mind, and to a great extent the nation rallied around them.

A lot of questions were asked that ultimately revealed the solutions required to place our men on the moon. This mission gave our nation a common purpose, allowing Americans to focus on something bigger than individual needs. It promoted optimism, inspiring the collective vision of accomplishing the impossible, while embodying Kennedy's message to the people of America: "Ask not what your country can do for you—ask what you can do for your country." Neil Armstrong was not alone that summer day in 1969 when he took a giant step for humankind—we were there with him.

Of course you do not have all the answers at the onset—no one does. What is important is that you understand you never will stretch yourself beyond your present experience until you envision something outside the boundaries of your current existence. It is said that necessity is the mother of all invention. What do you demand of yourself and the world around you? What is necessary in your life?

Start asking yourself, and when you come up with the answers, fixate on them. Then begin seeking the support you require to achieve your dreams. Despite the resistance you may initially face, you will find the answers and the support you seek!

Be in Touch with Your Feelings

As you define your objectives, draft a note as to how you envision them upon their completion. What do they look like, and how do you feel having accomplished them? Focus intently on the way you feel. Feelings play a critical role in what and how you project.

Lynn Grabhorn, author of *Excuse Me, Your Life Is Waiting — The Astonishing Power of Feelings*, does an incredible job of elaborating on the power associated with the way we feel at any given moment about any particular subject, and the circumstances or results we attract. Grabhorn tells the story of how she learned to *feel* her desires into being. She speaks of the "law of attraction" — the premise being that all things within our world are composed of energy — *everything*...you and I, right down to our thoughts. Energy is vibrating. All things being energy, all things are vibrating. Grabhorn points out that modern-day physicist have determined energy and matter are one.

We can logically conclude everything vibrates, although at a different rate. And because everything vibrates, whether you see it or not, it is energy. Grabhorn states, "...It's high time we woke up to the fact that we are electromagnetic beings tripping around with this mind-boggling capacity to magnetize into our lives whatever in the world we desire by controlling the feelings that come from our thoughts." [1]

I highly recommend you read *this book!*

Feeling Empowered?

Our feelings either empower us or render us powerless. Remember Jim Rohn's list of things to do and how he emphasizes that part of the fun is checking them off as you complete them? When you are having fun and witnessing your progress, how do you feel?

After having progressed with your coaching sessions, how do you feel given you have initiated the development of your plans—empowered or disempowered? You should feel more empowered than before, and as a result generating positive vibrations that in turn attract positive circumstances. Remember the Beach Boys and their song "Good Vibrations"? Their upbeat lyrics "I'm pickin' up good vibrations" have some scientific merit to them. The more you research this and the more you practice implementing empowering principles, the more you will believe and witness the benefits in your life.

I hope you are passionate about something in your life... perhaps a hobby, your work, a relationship, anything that will allow you to relate passion to enthusiasm. The word *enthusiasm* is

---

[1] Lynn Grabhorn, Excuse Me, Your Life Is Waiting—The Astonishing Power of Feelings, (Hampton Roads Publishing Company, Inc., 2000), 13.

derived from the Greek word *Entheos,* meaning "inspired from God." This just may explain the power we derive from doing something we are enthusiastic about. This also explains why enthusiasm attracts the attention of others, often generating the support required to accomplish the task at hand.

Your List of Things to Do

By now you should have developed a list of things to do, and visualized the end result you desire. Your list should be posted in a conspicuous place. Your dreams are taking on a new reality, and the process of nurturing them can be as rewarding as the prize itself. Your list may still be somewhat intimidating but this is not unusual. In fact, if you are not experiencing butterflies, your aspirations may be a bit too conservative.

Now you are ready to begin assessing what you will need to accomplish your objectives. You may require capital to get your dreams off the ground — capital you may not have. But the money exists somewhere. The key is in determining how you are going to attract it. Ask aloud, "Where will I find the money?" I am not joking with you. Ask the universe for some assistance. The answers will come. Although your request may first appear unreasonable, you have at least taken the steps to align yourself with your objective and retraced the trail blazed by the more formidable creative geniuses of our time. Stretch your imagination; you may require further education — formal or informal — to acquire the knowledge necessary to attain your dreams.

Peruse your local library or bookstore for books providing insight related to the subject of your interest. You will find how-to books pertaining to every topic imaginable. There can be considerable benefit in consulting with an expert. Remember the value of mirroring the masters—doing so will likely save you a substantial amount of time and money. Accept you will likely be required to make some form of sacrifice in order for you to attain your dreams. Once you have determined the price you will have in exchange, you may discover you do not really want it as much as you thought

Harness Your Stress

You are going to have to work to get where you want to be. Stress, while frequently viewed as a negative byproduct of life, almost always accompanies growth. You are likely stressed out about all you have to do or stressing over what you have failed to accomplish. The only way to control the stress in your life is by learning how to harness it. Stress is not *all* bad. Stress can give you a lift. A plane cannot fly without it. The very resistance or friction is the same component that in turn provides the lift necessary for flight; eliminate the resistance and you fall back to earth.

Is the resistance you may encounter going to be any worse than the stress you are experiencing in not having what you want? Make sure you are honest with yourself and become really clear with where you stand. When you are uncomfortable with remaining as you are, use the discomfort to propel toward your dreams.

Mind Your Thinking

Most of us find ourselves discouraged from time to time. When you feel this way, take a break, do something fun, change your environment — at least temporarily. Release your negative thoughts, telling the voice of pessimism to be silenced. Consider altering your focus. Negative thinking is burdensome, and the best way to overcome it is to take action. Put the principles you have learned thus far to the test.

Refer to your to-do list. Perhaps there is something you have been putting off acquiring because you were not quite sure how you were going to afford it. Before you get started, here are some ground rules: (1) You cannot finance it. (2) You cannot draw from your savings, checking, or mattress. You must find a way for what you desire to find its way to you. Here are some suggestions: Trade something for it, such as your services or something you already own, or have it gifted to you. Use your imagination, beginning with a clear mental image of attaining your desired objective. This process is no secret. It is the law of attraction, and it is as real as the law of gravity. We get what we focus on, although some things require more time and a greater intensity of focus than others.

Some time ago my wife and I were residing in Las Vegas, where I owned and operated a business. Late one afternoon, after having recently rearranged the living room at my wife's request, I had a vision of an upright piano positioned against the wall. I previously contemplated purchasing a piano; however, I had not followed through. On this particular day I found myself inspired to do so. I announced to my wife I was going to find a piano for our home. She did not appear to be thrilled at the prospect of an additional expenditure.

"Look, buddy," she said, "we have just paid off all of our debt, and I am not interested in taking on another payment!"

After briefly considering my options, I proposed I find a way to acquire a new or previously owned piano in exceptionally good condition without having to deplete our savings or go into debt.

"Would this be acceptable?" I asked.

"Sure, and good luck," she responded.

It already occurred to me we had a business trade account with a positive balance of nine thousand dollars, which we typically accessed for entertainment, travel accommodations, and so forth. Certainly, there had to be a music store among the group's members or someone within the group who would be interested in trading a piano that had been gathering dust in their own home. I boldly announced to my wife, "Within two weeks we will have a new piano."

I could see the piano, clear as day, sitting there against the wall in our living room. I had now announced to my wife and the universe my intent. I then wrote a note to myself in my daily planner to contact the trade group. The following day I did just that. There were no music stores enrolled with the group, but sure enough, they were able to direct me to a couple of businesses in the network that had a piano they were looking to trade. When the opportune moment presented itself, I drove across town to see the first piano. It must have been fifty years old and spent the better part of those years in an elementary school. It was not what I was looking for. I pressed on, only to find my disappointment duplicated at the next stop—the second piano was worst than the first. Neither of these pianos were what I had envisioned, and if this meant I was going to have to wait, then so be it.

I was disappointed and discouraged at first, but I remembered the importance of demonstrating faith. I clearly knew what I wanted and had made it known. My motives were pure, and most important, my family and I deserved it. I knew the piano I wanted would present itself in good time. Though it might not come to me as easily as I had thought, it would come. I chose to focus on my abundance, thanking God for all my family and I had been blessed with. Having done this, I released the outcome and turned my attention back to my business.

You may be wondering why I would decide to give up so easily. Believe me, I had not given up! I was simply abiding by the very principles and laws I have been espousing from the onset of our sessions together. I knew what I wanted, I announced my intent to the universe and to someone I respected, I made a notation of what I was to do, I acted on it, I focused on my blessings (my abundance), and finally, I released the outcome.

It is often enough to plant the seed; do not compact it in your desperation. When we relax, we are inclined to function more harmoniously with the world around us. I once again refer to the words of Napoleon Hill: "The moment you commit and quit holding back, all sorts of unforeseen incidents, meetings, and material assistance will rise up to help you. The simple act of commitment is a powerful magnet for help."

There are times in our lives when letting go of the outcome is exactly what we need to do. Have faith. The opportunity you are seeking will present itself. We tend to be impatient, and our anxiety drives away the very thing we are pursuing. What we want remains at arm's length until we are ready to appreciate our union. God, the universe, or however you want to refer to this magnificent force, wants you to live in abundance. Abundance is first and foremost, a state of mind.

I did not realize it at the time, but far more important to me than acquiring the piano was the lesson I was about to learn. Within two weeks of the declaration I had made to my wife, I called upon a prospective client—a young married couple who were moving into their new home. Upon my arrival I found them still unloading their belongings from the moving van. I could not help but notice the unmistakable shape of a piano draped in moving blankets. I asked who played. The wife responded she did, though she hated it. Her parents had purchased the piano new, eight years prior, and had forced her to enroll in lessons. She confessed she rarely played and had only accepted the piano at the insistence of her parents. I asked if I might look at it, stating I had been considering a piano for my family. It was like new, with an upright cabinet in a cherry wood finish. Could this be the opportunity I had been awaiting?

Without further discussion, I was invited into their home. Over the next hour or two I reviewed with them the benefits of the products my company provided. Both the husband and wife liked what I was offering, and they really wanted to move forward. However, having considered the substantial debt they had recently incurred, the wife said they would have to hold off for the time being.

Opportunity had presented itself, and I was a step ahead. I asked the couple if they had ever considered selling the piano; they had not. I asked them that if they were to consider selling it, what they thought it might be worth. They threw out a reasonable price, and I asked them if they would be interested in selling it to me. They were, and we subsequently came to an agreement, allowing me to accept the piano in trade toward their acquisition. The remaining balance covered my hard costs, and the piano constituted my profit. We both had what we wanted!

I will never forget the look on my wife's face when the piano was placed in the very room where I had made my declaration two weeks before. What is most exciting is that this was merely the beginning of a series of events that would reveal just how powerful the simplest thoughts can be.

This is an exciting prospect, isn't it? We truly possess the power to align ourselves with the elements and thus, with the energy and vibration of all living things. What is possible when you and I become aligned with the universal matter itself? We have simply been failing to recognize that we are already aligned and always have been.

It is Elementary

I realize I may be asking you to stretch your current paradigm. Stretch! Consider that history has demonstrated time and again how little we truly understand. Only recently did we identify the existence of bacteria and viruses. Electricity has always existed, and yet our ability to harness it is relatively new. The weather has mystified our species since the beginning of time. Now we forecast it. We have gained new perspectives that would astonish Galileo and Copernicus. Just because we fail to understand something today does not mean will not understand it in the future.

How will our children's children view the works of our generation? I hope we will be recognized for our willingness to move beyond what we deemed reasonable and remembered for the courage we demonstrated in pursuing the unreasonable. It is time we accept accountability to the stewardship of this planet, and our responsibility not only to the welfare of our generation but also for the welfare of generations to come.

Revisit your lifetime list of things to do, and include a number of contributions you intend to make to your community, your nation, and your world. Your efforts will have a far-reaching effect, likely greater than you may ever know. Expand your thinking and stretch your imagination until it becomes uncomfortable. You will then witness your potential as never before.

Session 7 Summary

- There is a price for everything, including remaining as you are.
- Plan for success.
- We think in pictures, so paint a Rembrandt.
- Visualize living your dreams.
- Feelings play a critical role in what we project.
- Become very clear on what you want. Make sure you want it for the right reasons, and then make your declaration to the universe.

Your Exercises for the Week

1. Determine the price you will have to pay for remaining as you are.
2. Determine the price you will likely pay for implementing the changes you desire.
3. Review your to-do list. Make sure you have detailed your activities for the week.
4. Pay close attention to the pictures you are creating when communicating with others.
5. Practice daily visualizing your desired life.
6. Observe the way you are feeling at any given moment and the universal response to what you are projecting.

7. Remember to select something you want to accomplish. Put the principles to the test. Give the universe some time.

Session Review

_____
_____
_____
_____
_____
_____
_____
_____
_____
_____
_____
_____
_____
_____
_____
_____
_____
_____
_____
_____
_____
_____
_____
_____
_____
_____
_____
_____

SESSION 8
TAKE MASSIVE AND IMMEDIATE ACTION

Welcome to Session Eight with your personal coach. You are now three quarters of the way through your twelve-week program. The principles you have been exposed to thus far provide the foundation for those to come. Together they will grant you unprecedented power to create the life of your dreams.

By now you have likely gained a clearer perspective as to who you really are, what you like and dislike, your strengths and weaknesses, and so forth. You have identified what comprises your inner core as well as the ideals and qualities you value, permitting yourself to quickly assess what aligns or conflicts with the individual you have chosen to become. You have forgiven yourself and the transgressions of others. You choose to live in the moment, freed from the past and possessing a positive anticipation of what the future holds in store for you.

You have permitted yourself to dream without constraint, no longer festered by the doomsayers who would predict your failure. Instead, you find yourself focused on the promise afforded you by your optimism. You now choose to think and act from a mindset of abundance rather than of scarcity. You have announced your intent to the universe and to someone who will encourage you in your undertaking.

You have planned for your success and determined your readiness to pay the price, creating the room in your life necessary for the gifts you are about to receive. It is time to act on the decisions you have made. Nothing will hold you back because you have at last come to recognize that you are unstoppable. This is a glorious day, one to always treasure.

Now Take Action!

"I do not believe in a fate that falls on men however they act; but I do believe in a fate that falls on them unless they act."—Buddha

"The wise man in the storm prays to God, not for safety from danger but for the deliverance from fear. It is the storm within that endangers him, not the storm without." —Ralph Waldo Emerson

The fear you may have once succumbed to has been defeated by the action you are taking; your focus has been redirected to the very thing you are working to accomplish. Fear equates to paralysis as action equates to liberation. Every time you encounter fear you will remember that the way to overcome it is to do the very thing your fear would have you suppress. In the words of Franklin D. Roosevelt, "The only thing we have to fear is fear itself."

There will be times after you take action in your personal or your professional life when you will find yourself wondering if the results will ever materialize. You may find yourself putting forth a great deal of energy and resources, yet experiencing little or no return. You may feel the fear beginning to set in. You may find yourself questioning your methods, your beliefs, and even your worthiness. Relax and ease off for a little while, re-evaluate your methods, and use a fresh approach. Whatever you do, do not give up. You may find it necessary to alter your strategy, but do not give up!

Have you ever attempted to assemble something that just would not fit together the way it should, and in your efforts you ended up breaking it? I have, only to discover I had misjudged or misread the instructions. This usually occurs when I am tired and as a result, easily frustrated. I would have been much better off to temporarily place my project on hold and returned to it another day.

When you are working diligently to achieve an objective that remains elusive, it will likely be in your best interest to step back from the project. As I have stated, the answer may be as simple as discovering that your timing was premature. There is a great deal more to what I am saying here than many readers may appreciate. I am not sure I understand the complexity of it myself, but I have witnessed it at work.

Earlier I mentioned Robert Wiegand, my managing agent when I worked for Monarch Life Insurance Company. I remember Robert emphasizing the importance of prospecting. Prospecting is nothing complicated; it is simply contacting people you may or may not know and determining if they are possible candidates for the products or services your business provides. It may sound easy, yet it is the most dreaded task in the direct-sales industry. It is often referred to as cold calling—likely for the cold reception some salespeople experience. You do not have to be in direct sales to know what a cold reception is. Each of us has experienced it in the grocer's isle at the supermarket. Some people cannot find it in themselves to be nice even if you saved them from a burning building. Fortunately, they are few; nonetheless, they can discourage the most positive among us.

The very mention of prospecting can instill terror in the hearts of those new to sales. Even veterans often find themselves hesitant to prospect as they should, and as a result they often place prospecting on the back burner, finding busy work to keep them occupied. The fear of prospecting is unfounded. A surefire way to overcome this fear is to do the very prospecting you are afraid of. In time you will discover it is not only a great way to open doors, it is also a fantastic way to develop friendships. Knock and the door will be opened. You have to knock. The individual who takes the initiative takes the prize.

Like most who are new to sales, I dreaded contacting people, whether I knew them or not. The very thought of doing so left me nauseous. I turned my performance around in time by realizing prospecting was nothing to be afraid of. In retrospect, overcoming this fear became the driving force of my success. In the midst of my tempestuous insurance career under the direction of Robert Wiegand, I learned something I will never forget.

Robert taught me that prospecting was simply a form of taking action—putting forth the effort to promote an end result. He knew the action of prospecting triggered some type of unexplained response from the universe. When we take action, the results we seek frequently do not materialize as a direct result of the actions taken. Say you are making calls each day to business owners within an industry you are targeting, and it just does not seem to be working. Out of nowhere someone calls, looking for the product or service you provide. You did not necessarily contact them; it may be a referral or a random call—or so we think. It happens all the time. It is as if the universe rewards those who are putting forth the effort; it just seems to work this way...which brings us once again to the law of attraction. The universe does, in fact, reward effort. For every action there is an equal and proportionate reaction. We reap what we sow; isn't it karmic?

The law of attraction has made all the difference in my life. The bigger I allow myself to think, the grander my opportunities become. The more I accept I am deserving of great things, the easier it is to accomplish them; we do not come by much in our lives that we do not feel we deserve. The more deserving we feel, the more we are likely to demand life meets our expectations. I am not suggesting we approach life arrogantly or with a self-centered attitude of entitlement. I am merely proposing we break beyond any doctrine claiming we are unworthy of achieving greatness. Humility has its place, but to live boldly with the spirit of an adventurer is far more fulfilling.

Historically it is the bold individuals who unlock the true potential of humanity. As George Bernard Shaw stated, "The reasonable man adapts himself to the world. The unreasonable man persists in trying to adapt the world to himself. Therefore, all progress depends on the unreasonable man." This may remind you of Thomas Edison's philosophy about approaching a problem: Once we have exhausted all the reasonable options we have, we will be forced to investigate unreasonable options. We can be assured the solution is just around the corner.

I hope you have come to conclude, like Thomas Edison, Jay Greenberg, and Dustin Hoffman, that you are no longer willing to settle for anything less than the dreams to which you aspire. You understand God is as determined to grant you the life you desire as you are determined to create it. This is the law of attraction; you can cooperate with it or not. Your victory is strictly up to you. I hope you will find encouragement in knowing the good you ask for will be granted, though not always as you had envisioned it. Prepare to find yourself marveling at the way in which life unfolds.

"Would any of you who are fathers give your son a stone when he asks for bread? Or would you give him a snake when he asks for fish? As bad as you are, you know how to give good things to your

children. How much more, then, will your Father in heaven give good things to those who ask of him!" [1]

I believe the accurate way to interpret this verse is that we make horrific mistakes. We do things at times that are undoubtedly destructive; other times we do a great deal of good. If someone frequently tells you how evil you are, watch out. You would be wise to question their motives. You may have witnessed someone posing as a spiritual or religious leader who is constantly emphasizing how corrupt and evil humankind is. Get away from them as fast as possible. What we need to focus on is how decent we are. By abiding the laws governing the universe, we draw out the good that exists.

The biblical account of creation states humankind was created in the image of God. Like God, we possess free will. Unfortunately, we frequently use it to create a great deal of hardship for others and ourselves. Man can be as evil at times as he can be good. The fact is we collectively do far more good than evil. Certainly each of us has committed some act that does not make us proud, but most people are inherently good despite the error of their ways.

The verse above, as I interpret it, is intended as a testament to the kindness and generosity of God and his ready willingness to grant the blessings we ask. More than anything, it affirms the physical law of attraction. **We attract what we focus on.** Introduce

---

[1] Matthew 7:9–11, Good News Bible, the American Bible Society, New York, 1966.

faith—our acceptance that the good we ask for is drawn to us through the act of asking and in believing what we have asked for will come to pass. Our doubt comes from thinking that what we have asked for may not come to pass, and our resulting focus is one of scarcity.

Bingo! We get what we focus on. Subtle as it is, the law of attraction is real and extremely powerful. Yes, we do not always get what we ask for, but by no means does this imply the law of attraction is inconsistent. *We* are inconsistent with the thoughts we project and or what we desire may not be everything we perceive it to be; thus it is not in our best interest that our ambition is fulfilled.

Have you ever really wanted something so desperately that it consumed your every thought? Then, when you finally got it, you discovered it did not provide the enjoyment you had anticipated it would. Most of us have! At times we have found ourselves wondering what in heaven's name we had been thinking. When this happens, you may want to consider that although it did not turn out the way you had hoped, there was something to be learned from your experience. It may be that what you had wanted was granted in order for you to grow spiritually. Sometimes it is an unpleasant experience, and we might best be described as childish, casting blame on the universe for the pain we find ourselves suffering.

As we come to understand and accept our responsibility for where we find ourselves, we can begin to adjust our thinking and behavior so it aligns with the physical laws that govern us. I compare this to swimming against a riptide. As any lifeguard will tell you, this is not something you want to do. You are no match for the current. However, when you understand the physics at work, remain calm, and swim parallel to the shore until you are free from the outgoing tide. The ocean surf will become your ally.

Appreciate What You Have

For those of you with children, it is probably fair to say you will always desire what is best for them. Most parents do. We are inclined to give them as much as we can—things we as children may have done without. If you have raised your own children I will wager that somewhere along the path you have given your child a gift you were ecstatic about, only to witness the child complain. How did you feel when this happened? I wonder how quick you were to offer the child something else. Did you question whether the child had yet developed the maturity to appreciate your efforts and sacrifice?

You undoubtedly realized your child likely had little or no concept of what was required on your behalf. Did you consider the opportunity to permit the child to wallow in his disappointment? This may be the greatest gift we as parents could give to our children at such a time. The gift of appreciation is a gift that keeps giving for a lifetime. As parents we are the first line of defense for our children, and we are often the first to promote their disabilities by failing to teach them how to live in abundance.

God, or the universe, will increase our blessings when we come to appreciate what we already have, however little this may appear to be. Take a good look at what you have. I hope there are many things you are grateful for. Focus on them, praise God for them, thank the Universe, and witness a greater abundance flowing ever so freely your way.

Think Positively

Granted, everything you will accomplish begins with the way you think, but if you expect that your thoughts alone will create the life you desire, think again. You better be prepared to take action when you want results. I know this is difficult for many, particularly at the onset; yet I assure you once you are in motion, you will not remain alone, and it will become easier. Your resistance can likely be attributed to your fear of pain. We often find ourselves associating more pain with changing our present practices than remaining as we are. If this is true for you, you had better get a handle on it because nothing significant is going to happen until you put forth the effort.

Remember, when you step up to the plate and take action, the action you take may not be directly responsible for creating the outcome you desire. Stay the course and remain in motion. The physical laws of the universe will in no way reward you should you choose to sit your sorry behind back down. If you think this sounds harsh, it cannot compare to a stagnant life filled with despair. You know what you have always wanted to do...now just do it!

Begin Now

As soon as you have completed this session, find it in yourself to do something constructive — anything that will bring you closer to accomplishing your objective. We must all begin somewhere, and if you find yourself struggling, ask someone for assistance. When we ask, we receive. Sometimes we have to keep asking. Whatever you do, do not stop at the first sign of resistance. This is where we can learn from our children. They do not give up easily, and they possess the endless energy to play forever! When you finally decide to do what you have always wanted to do, you will find it is more like playing than working. You too will have more energy than you know what to do with!

Now refer to your list of things to do. Begin with your "A" priorities, making sure you check them off as you complete them. This is truly a great way to maintain a positive attitude as you move from one project to the next. Practice this daily, and you will be drawn closer and closer to your objective until you finally attain it. Do not be surprised if you feel a bit let down once you have achieved your goal. The process of creating is frequently far more fulfilling than basking in the success of our accomplishments.

The more you do, the more you will find yourself driven to do. The more you present yourself to the world, the more the world will present to you.

We Are Never Alone

One of the most exciting epiphanies I have ever experienced was in discovering we are not alone. How liberating it is to come to the realization that the universe will deliver what we need, when we need it!

In the mid 1990s I was the vice president of sales and one of four principal shareholders of a collection company. One December I was scheduled to spend the first two weeks of the month conducting business in Southern California. My telemarketing team was responsible for scheduling my meetings with prospective commercial accounts prior to my arrival. I appeared booked with a respectable number of qualified accounts. I love California in December, and looked forward to a break from Salt Lake City's winter.

This particular December did not greet me as favorably as years past: the weather was miserable. It rained and then rained some more. To add to my frustration with the weather, my scheduled meetings were falling miserably short of my expectations. I had failed to transact a sale in six consecutive days — an accomplishment uncharacteristic of my performance. I was quickly becoming discouraged. Disheartened or not, I had a few days remaining, and I was not about to give up! It is when we least feel like doing something, and press forth regardless, that we experience our greatest successes.

On the Tuesday of my second week of fighting traffic and hydroplaning, I called on a Christian book publishing company. My partner, the CEO of our company, had been fixated on capturing the company's business for some time. He was convinced I possessed the magic necessary to entice them away from our largest competitor. I attribute this to my desire to serve others before myself. Put others first and you will be a step closer to becoming the master of your world.

I failed to woo the book publisher from our competitor. They had a substantial need for the type of service we provided, and I am convinced we offered a superior program. They did not t see it that way. I came away having to respect that they had a strong personal relationship with our competitor's representative, and as such demonstrated an admirable desire to remain loyal to him. He had served them well for many years. I would have loved to have learned his name; he is the type of individual I want working for me.

Seven days of business, nine consecutive days away from home, and I had struck out with the first truly qualified account I had met. My self-esteem had certainly taken a beating. I found myself once again navigating the perilous interstate system of Southern California. As I made my way south, I was compelled to visit the gravesite of my father, something I had never done in the thirty-four years since his death.

I remembered my mother mentioning the name and general location of the cemetery where my father had been laid to rest. After a quick inquiry with the cellular directory service, I had the number and address in hand. I arrived at about 4 p.m. I borrowed an umbrella from the gate attendant and drove the winding road through the hills in search of my father's resting site. I remember thinking to myself how beautiful the cemetery was and wondering what had taken me so long to visit it despite the countless opportunities that had been previously presented.

Once in the general vicinity of my destination, I parked the car and proceeded on foot down a long embankment. I slipped and tumbled a short distance down the saturated hillside, spraining my ankle. I have little doubt I could have been heard a mile away cursing the rain, my unprofitable business trip, and my father, all in a single breath. I was managing quite well to feel sorry for myself.

Hobbling around, I desperately sought the granite marker that bore his name. It was growing dark, and my time was running short when I finally concluded this had not been worth my effort. After all, what had my father ever done for me? I turned my attention to my car (which was located up the hill from where I was standing), only to find myself staring at my father's name engraved on the monument directly in front of me. I fell instantly to my knees, telling him of my wife and children—their names, ages, and all they have meant to me. Then, without reservation or hesitation, I told him I loved him and I had missed him. Most importantly, I let him know I had forgiven him for the decision he had made to take his life three decades prior.

I suppose there is much in life we will never understand. On this day I learned something so critical it would change my life forever. I gathered the strength to stand and walk back up the hillside to my car, where I brushed grass from my clothing and drove back to the gatehouse, returning the umbrella to the attendant. His expression, or perhaps his demeanor, revealed that my appearance must have provided some testimonial to what I had just experienced. He kindly wished me well, and I was on my way.

Once again I intended to return to the condominium, but as I entered the freeway I heard a voice. I could have sworn it was audible. It reminded me I had one remaining meeting I was to keep. I was so startled I actually responded aloud, "No way. I am in no shape to meet with anybody right now!" To my utter amazement, I once again heard the voice, this time commanding me, "Go anyway."

I am not accustomed to having such conversations with myself. I was skeptical. I was also intrigued or perhaps intimidated just enough not to ignore my instructions. So I referenced my planner, and sure enough I had overlooked one remaining meeting that I had been scheduled to make, in person, anytime between the hours of 8 a.m. and 6 p.m. As a rule, a meeting scheduled in this manner did not typically constitute the best of prospects, and in good traffic the business was located at least fifteen minutes away. My watch read 5:20 p.m. I did not have much time, and were traffic conditions unfavorable I would not make it at all. Despite everything I decided to take my chances. I had no choice. The voice had been too compelling.

There Are No Coincidences

As it turned out the traffic was light, and I arrived at my destination with minutes to spare. I entered what was a large veterinarian hospital, and approached the front counter in the lobby. The young woman who greeted me confirmed she was the office manager and had been expecting my arrival. She asked if I could wait for a few minutes while she continued to assist the onslaught of customers who were picking up their pets prior to the clinic's closing. Between distractions, I would have the opportunity to ask a few questions pertaining to their needs.

It quickly became apparent my services would provide the solution they were seeking. The office manager agreed with my recommendation. She then yielded the final decision to the clinic's head physician, asking for a moment so she might brief him and make an appropriate introduction for me. A few minutes later I found myself in the company of a tall, energetic man who possessed an engaging personality. Rather than using the formality of his title he introduced himself as Frank.

I summarized the findings of my discovery with him. He concurred with the office manager. At this, I was free to make my recommendation for the hospital to Frank. He was pleased with what I had presented and asked me what I would do considering the options we had just reviewed. As always, I offered my honest opinion, basing my recommendations on the interests of the practice rather than on my own interests. People sense sincerity. As you have likely already assumed, we did business. This account alone was enough to justify my trip.

There is something far greater to this story than the business transacted, something money cannot buy. I had yet to identify what it was, when I found myself compelled to do something I would typically refrain from doing—apologizing for my appearance, and choosing to share with Frank my experience at the cemetery. He listened attentively as I recounted my story. Then he asked a rather interesting question. I answered the best way I knew how, taking out a piece of paper and offering an example of a written exercise that had been shared with me two years earlier at a life development program. Before I could complete my outline, Frank asked for the paper and pen, and to my surprise, finished what I had initiated. I was astonished at the coincidence. As it turns out, Frank had attended the same program. It was then that I truly began to understand there are no coincidences — only a universal intent to make introductions to opportunities for us to learn, grow, and prosper.

Frank and I exchanged a few ideas and opinions over the next half hour. Then he paused momentarily, looked straight into my eyes, and said, "Mark, as soon as the opportunity presents itself, call your wife and share with her what you accomplished today. I want you to know how much I admire your openness and your courage." I thanked him, and at that we shook hands and parted.

We are never alone — never. We are all part of a universal consciousness that makes the introductions vital to our well-being. For those of you who desire to align yourself consistently with this power, you must allow yourself to be vulnerable. We are afraid of becoming vulnerable; thus, we avoid being too open. We hold back and remain reserved so we can avoid the unfavorable judgment of others. Remember this: you will not accomplish anything worthwhile without finding yourself ridiculed at times. There are too many foolish people who cannot wait to criticize others for having the courage to take risks. Their criticism is an attempt to hide their own feelings of inadequacy. Do not let their fear become yours. Be real with who you are and real with others. When we *are open and real, we connect with those who are also* open and real. Miraculous events become the ordinary.

Demonstrate Your Faith

Trust that your needs and desires will be met as you have asked, and they will be. Take action despite the opposition you may face, practice a little patience, and when the going gets tough, persist. I will always be grateful I found myself compelled to press forward on what had to be one of the most difficult days of my life.

There will be times when you work for extended periods without any observable results. Do not become discouraged should you find yourself having to change your path. There will likely be something, if not many things, you will learn. Now you can redirect yourself. Remember, there are occasions when we must travel for some distance before we can be certain it is not the path we had hoped for. Some seeds will take root, some will not. The critical lesson we must learn is that had we stood paralyzed in indecision at the fork in the road, choosing no path whatsoever, we would never have progressed at all.

It comes back to what I shared with you a number of sessions ago—the path to our success, more often than not, can be attributed to having experienced a succession of failures. Do not let the fear of striking out prevent you from stepping up to the plate! You will never hit a home run by refusing to swing. You have undoubtedly heard it before but it is worth mentioning again: Edison failed countless times before finding a workable solution for his light-bulb. Everyone who has accomplished anything remarkable has failed before they finally got it right. Every exceptional individual has had others discourage them. These are the lessons we all must learn as we progress along the path to achieving excellence. If you are not making mistakes, you are not striving to accomplish the remarkable. If others are not criticizing you, at least periodically, you are acting far too reasonable.

For those who think having faith means living without opposition, think again. Faith would not be necessary without opposition. Having faith promotes the strength, endurance, and insight you need to defeat the opposition. Your faith will lead to the introductions and circumstances necessary to facilitate your success. If there is not something tangible to be gained, there is something to be learned. As I have stated, the value of the gifts we seek is often surpassed by the value of the lesson itself. A wonderful book, *The Celestine Prophecy*, by James Redfield, expands on this. Redfield's book will leave you contemplating the circumstances you had once written off to coincidence.

Not long ago I attended a real estate investment seminar conducted by a gentleman named Bill Gatten from California. Gatten loves to share stories and is adept at doing so. He is exceptional at granting the listener insight into the effectiveness of the principles which promote success. His charismatic personality conveys his sincerity and passion for what he teaches. Gatten shares the "There are no coincidences" theory in a manner that is both relatable and believable. He presents the physics/metaphysical supposition that all matter interacts or cooperates in relationship to what can ultimately be reduced to a mathematical process (living by the numbers so-to-speak).

What caught my attention was Gatten's reference to *synchronicity*, the term he uses to describe a number of so-called coincidences, aligning sequentially to create a rather remarkable event. Most of us can recall some experience that may be defined as such. Reflect on your life. You have likely witnessed synchronicity at work. I have experienced numerous such events. I say this confidently because they have become almost commonplace as I have embraced the principles I share with you. As a result I recognize these events for what they are—a gift for choosing to live in a conscious state.

Anything worthwhile requires practice, including remaining truly conscious of our environment. As the muscles within our bodies respond to exercise, so does the mind and spirit. Neglect any among them, and they will atrophy. The process of living successfully is quite similar. Leading a truly abundant life, one that provides for creativity, fulfillment, and joy, requires we regularly exercise our mind, body, and spirit. Though there are times that call for us to sacrifice in one or more of these areas, we will find that should we remain imbalanced for prolonged periods, something will give. All things considered, we must remain in motion—improving, growing, and creating—or we will find ourselves deteriorating. There is no in between.

Take action in your life now. You will not be alone, I assure you. Visualize the end result you desire. Do not worry about how you are going to complete the task at hand. Take a step forward in faith, and commit yourself to accomplishing something remarkable. The universe will rise up to assist you in your endeavor. You are going to make a great discovery about yourself in the coming weeks!

Session 8 Summary

- Take massive and immediate action!
- Release the outcome in prayer.
- Appreciate the gift of life.
- Follow through—you must do your part.
- Some seeds will not take root, some will. Plant many.
- You are not alone.

Your Exercises for the Week

1. Pull out your prioritized to-do list and act now.
2. Ask yourself what you can do. Do not worry how you're going to go about it.
3. Give some thought to what you can do to move closer to your objective. Be patient. Great things take time!
4. Keep a log of the ideas that come to you, the actions you take, and the results you derive.
5. Be aware of circumstances that at first may appear random and record where they lead you. Over time, you will recognize the importance of these events. Events you would have once considered coincidental will reveal themselves to be anything but.

6. Continue to plan your days using the prioritized to-do list.

Session Review

_____

_____

_____

_____

_____

_____

_____

_____

_____

_____

_____

_____

_____

_____

_____

_____

_____

_____

_____

_____

_____

_____

_____

_____

_____

OPPORTUNITIES ABOUND

Welcome to Session Nine with your personal coach. Having completed your exercises from our last session together, you should now find yourself taking action on the plans you have developed over the last number of weeks. Feels great, doesn't it? As you are taking action, you are likely encountering more opportunities than you had previously imagined possible.

Consider the Impossible

Something exceptionally remarkable occurs when you adhere to the process that has been outlined thus far: you witness your world begin to expand and you see opportunities you had never before recognized. It really is as simple as I have stated. Choose to change your thinking, and you will begin to change your life.

Hopefully you have had enough of things as they are and you are committed to get where you truly desire to be. Until recently you have been seeking out reasonable options to attain the life of your dreams. The problem, as you have undoubtedly discovered, is the majority of reasonable people do not get to where they want to be. And the majority typically influences what we perceive to be reasonable and unreasonable with respect to the actions we choose to take. The tragedy is that far too many of us succumb to the will of the majority.

We are all pretty much familiar with the phrase "outside the box," which suggests we transcend our own conforming thinking. I propose we transcend our minds periodically and ask ourselves how we might view something were we someone else. It is a great exercise! Here is an example: Select someone at random you would like to understand or perhaps emulate, and ask yourself how this person perceives the world. What possibilities exist for this person because of their thinking? Make a real effort to understand how this person views the world. How do their perceptions serve them in attaining what so few among us achieve? Choose people who have accomplished something you too would like to accomplish. What is it they understand about themselves, the world, and life in general that you are currently failing to recognize for yourself?

My experience as a personal coach has led me to conclude that the majority of us circle the solutions or opportunities we encounter, failing to recognize them, even though they were present all the while. Perhaps the reason those who achieve remarkable results do so because they see their goal as being possible, and they are not afraid to be unreasonable in how they go about achieving it. To move past the mundane, look beyond yourself and your circumstances, and reconsider what you have thought impossible to this point. Think big! Listen closely to me. If you want to quit living from paycheck to paycheck, for example, then see yourself achieving the big project, closing the deal of a lifetime, or building your own business. Examine how you feel each month with just barely getting by. It is a miserable feeling, isn't it? Whether you are living this way currently or not, if you were not born into great wealth, you have most likely experienced what it is like to worry about money. The way to quit worrying about money is to quit worrying about money.

I remember when I used to say to myself each month I needed so much income this month to cover my bills. Sure enough I brought in the figure I had focused on—sometimes a little more, sometimes a little less. Either way I was amazingly consistent every month. Most of us operate from a position of need and so we find ourselves constantly in need. Then we perform within the scope of what we think we are worth. Those of you who are salaried do the same thing; you make the decision every month to remain employed as you are. Do not just brush this aside; it is really important you grasp this concept and internalize it if you are determined to live in abundance.

Most of us have been trained to believe we will be able to put our worries behind us when we have the money to live as we wish. The truth is we will create the money we need to live as we wish when we quit worrying about how we are going to make it and put our energy instead toward developing a better life. Money is not the solution; it is a tool. The solution lies in learning how to adjust your thinking so you become proficient in attracting the money necessary to achieve your dreams. When you keep focusing on the money you need, you are in effect asking the universe to meet your needs and your needs alone. I will bet were you to examine your life over the past few years you would tell me, "Mark, you're right. As

I reflect on my finances, I always seem to have what I need." It may barely be enough at times, and you are probably somewhat uncomfortable on occasion, but you would have to respond that the money presents itself almost miraculously just when you needed it most.

Raise the bar and incorporate your life's dreams with your needs. As I have told you, life will give you only what you demand of it. Instead of focusing each month on your needs, focus on your dreams; they are what you require to truly live. Life has so much more to offer us than simple sustenance; it is about fulfilling ourselves. Remember the words of Jay Greenberg: "I am going to be dead if I am not composing. I have to compose." Are you paying attention? Jay *needs* to compose; his dreams and needs are one in the same.

Go for It!

The way for any of us to progress beyond what we currently find ourselves doing is to first see ourselves doing it. Consider the time I acquired a $380,000, 5,200-square-foot residential property with only $1,250 out of pocket.

My wife, children, and I were living in a 3,200-square-foot, two-story English Tudor that we owned. Tresha and I really wanted a larger home for our family, yet it just did not appear to be financially feasible at the time. I was in the midst of a career move and we were feeling the economic impact. In all actuality we were in a world of hurt, and had I been reasonable I would never have considered attempting what I did. My desire was all consuming. I had to find a way to make peace with myself, and the only way I felt I could do this was to purchase the home I had been yearning for.

My fixation with acquiring a new home began when my wife and I hosted a party for a few friends. As we socialized in the kitchen, I became increasingly aware of what I did not like about our present home. Somehow it came up in conversation. I began describing the features I would like our new home to have. As the details of its design unfolded, I imagined myself standing in our new kitchen. Our conversation soon moved beyond the subject, but the seed had been planted deep within my psyche.

Now equipped with a clear visual image of what I desired, I needed to announce my intent. The following day, I told my wife I was going to find a home more appropriate for our family's needs. With her blessings, I expanded my list of things to do, prioritized, and began searching for the home I had envisioned. Though I had some ideas as to how I might finance my project, I was far from certain I would be successful, even if I was fortunate enough to find the home I was looking for.

In the coming days I invested a fair amount of time conducting my research. Considering that the residential real estate market was soft (particularly the high-end properties), it occurred to me I might find someone who was having difficulty selling his or her home. As logic would indicate, during poor market conditions, sellers are typically more flexible in offering terms. I had been exposed to some of the teachings of the contemporary real estate investment gurus and possessed some understanding of how to orchestrate a seller-carried purchase contract.

Over the next two weeks I searched the papers. To our good fortune, I responded to an advertisement describing a beautiful two-story mountain home available for lease. Located at the base of a canyon, this custom 5,200-square-foot home on a third of an acre featured five bedrooms, four bathrooms, two fireplaces, formal living room, formal dining room, large great room, game room, two decks, gorgeous fully landscaped yard, breathtaking views, and of course, the gourmet kitchen of our dreams.

I was not interested in leasing; yet I called nevertheless. After conversing with the owner, I learned he was eager to find a tenant. I set a time later that day to meet with him and see the home. Upon arriving, I found it was as striking as he described. The property, meticulously landscaped with sprawling lawns, was tucked amidst an abundance of pines, maples, and a variety of foliage. The views were sensational in every direction. It was as though I had found myself embraced by the mountains. In touring the interior I found the home to be all I had hoped for, including the kitchen which bore a remarkable resemblance to the culinary marvel I had described just two weeks before.

During my conversation with the owner I politely inquired as to his reasons for relocating. It turns out that he had lost control of the company he had founded some years before. Apparently there had been a change in the majority stockholders, and they had appointed a new CEO. The bottom line was that this man was out of work. Despite the hardship he was facing, his demeanor was remarkably pleasant. It was apparent he had already found closure and was resolved, if not content, in knowing he and his family would find their way to better days.

As I stated earlier, I was not interested in leasing the home. To my delight, during my visit with this gentleman I learned the home had recently been listed for sale. The soft real estate market had affected him just as it had so many. He could no longer sustain the mortgage, or he chose not to, so he had decided to lease it until market conditions improved, at which time he would place it back on the market for sale. This provided the perfect opportunity for me to introduce a solution he in all likelihood had not considered.

I informed him I was really looking to purchase rather than to lease. He asked me what I had in mind. I told him I had a home I had yet to place on the market, and the odds of me qualifying for a loan on his property before selling my home were in all likelihood nonexistent. I explained that I would, however, consider purchasing his home on contract. This appeared to capture his interest. The combined monthly payments of his first and second mortgages were more than I wanted to pay. He agreed to cover the difference each month for thirty-six months, at which time I would refinance and cash him out altogether. It appeared as though we had both found what we were looking for.

The following day Tresha accompanied me to the property, and to my delight she was as enthralled with its beauty as I was. We offered the seller $320,000 — $60,000 below what I had determined the true market value of the home to be based on the area's comparables. We placed only $1,250 down, conducted our inspection, ordered a title search, and closed on our purchase approximately six weeks from the date that I had announced my intent to purchase a new home.

A few months after taking occupancy, I learned the former owner had defaulted on the second mortgage, unable to keep his commitment to maintain the payments for thirty-six months, as he had agreed. By the time he filed bankruptcy and the property had moved into foreclosure, my wife and I purchased the second mortgage for approximately twelve cents on the dollar, refinanced the first, pulled out some money to pay off our debt and enjoyed our new home for the next seven years. It's a good thing I had not been thinking and acting reasonably!

Be Bold and Ask

Questions are the door to opportunity. When opportunities present themselves, we frequently lose out by hesitating to ask the questions that will ultimately provide the insight that can and often will make all the difference. We fail to ask questions for a number of reasons. Sometimes it is because we do not know the right questions to ask. Other times we do not want to appear stupid in the eyes of others. Perhaps we do not want to be overly assertive or seen by others as being aggressive. We may be afraid of being rejected, and heaven forbid we should find ourselves embarrassed at the foolish opinion of others.

Furthering your education may provide you with the answers to many of the questions pertinent to your field of interest. Education will also increase the probability that you will ask the questions likely to provide the quality answers you are seeking. As I have said before, you will find life works when you ask the right questions.

More wisdom is possessed in the questions we ask than in the answers we seek. Asking appropriate questions makes a big difference when pertaining to the quality of information you receive. It is also important you open your mind to that information. Never underestimate human intuition; it plays a significant role in providing for your success. As I have previously stated, we have access to a universal consciousness that will provide the insight and assistance we need to overcome the obstacles we will face. We need only ask!

I recommend you pray for guidance, and have faith that your prayers will be answered. For those who may be skeptical, I suggest you pray regardless. I hope that I do not offend anyone by being so direct. Understand I am convinced that prayer possesses, at minimum, the power to reach our subconscious mind, where seeds of inspiration and hope are planted. There is always a universal response to prayer, and it begins with you. I again emphasize that the blessings you ask for may not appear as you had envisioned. Be at peace with this, for they will in all likelihood surpass your expectations.

Many years ago I was struggling in my business, as well as in my personal life, and I found myself in a perpetual state of frustration. I was easily aggravated, frequently discouraged, and downright angry because I felt I had too much responsibility. My wife and I had three children and one on the way. I was running a young business and fulfilling multiple roles in the day-to-day operations. I am deeply saddened to say I was not particularly overjoyed with the prospect of another child at the time. The thought of all the additional responsibilities and financial demands of a newborn made me shutter. To make things worse, I was selfish and inconsiderate of my wife during the first few months of her pregnancy, giving little thought to what she was feeling. I know this was terrible of me, and I have long regretted my blindness and outright unappreciative response to the blessing this new life represented.

I finally turned to prayer, asking for guidance in hopes that I might find peace of mind with all that was troubling me. I also know my wife had been praying for me to awaken. Despite our prayers, for many days I resisted. In the midst of all our anxiety, my wife and I decided a change of scene might be in order. New surroundings can do wonders for one's perspective and promote a healthier attitude.

Tresha, the children, and I were off to San Diego to spend time with some dear friends. When we arrived in the city, we dropped into the local grocery store to pick up a few things we needed for the night's dinner. Our friends had invited us to stay with them for the weekend, and we decided to make dinner for everyone. It is not like us to show up empty-handed, particularly after having such a gracious invitation extended to us.

Moments after entering the store, Tresha was approached by a distinguished gentleman, many years her senior. The man leaned gently toward Tresha and complimented her on her three beautiful children. Then he said the most peculiar thing: "Your family is not yet whole. You must have one more child to make the total four, and then your family will be complete." He smiled warmly, turned, and walked away, vanishing as quickly as he had appeared.

Do angels really exist? If so, I imagine this man was one. "How did he know? How could he know?" we asked ourselves. After all, Tresha was barely a few months into her pregnancy and was not yet showing. No one could have known! Was this merely coincidental, or was it some sort of spiritual confirmation? Were we being advised by some higher consciousness as to the purpose this child would play in the completion of our family? All I know is that the son we would have turned out to be exactly what our family to be whole, just as this man had said. Some might say we would never have known the difference had he not been conceived. I can tell you we would have!

As you might imagine, I could not disregard what had happened. The experience was too strange, and I have been fortunate to have witnessed many times in my life when there was tremendous truth to the saying, "God works in mysterious ways." My apprehension subsided over the next few days. This experience presented me with a new perspective, and it soon moved me in the right direction. Incidentally, our newborn son required little work in comparison

193

to the blessings he provided us all. I cannot imagine life without him. I would not want to.

Do not spend your precious time worrying. As you have read, I have done my share during my lifetime, and it has only been in recent years that I have learned not to worry. I have finally come to appreciate the wisdom of my grandfather, who once told me that had he the opportunity to live his life again, he would not have wasted his time with worry—most of what he had worried about never came to pass. When we worry, it is frequently because we do not want to face the discomfort of dealing with the circumstances we fear. Yet our struggles often present the greatest opportunity for us to grow.

Have You Been Listening?

God speaks through us every day! The people we encounter may very well possess the message we are seeking and in turn, we may possess the message they have been awaiting. Ask for help when you find yourself isolated or uncertain of the direction you should take. It is amazing to witness the works that transpire. Pay close attention to the subtleties of even the briefest exchanges you are blessed with daily.

Through the Eyes of a Child

Not long after the birth of our son, I was invited by some dear friends to attend a course in personal development. I initially resisted. I can still remember expressing my frustration with life and how it was not measuring up to my expectations. There had to be something more to life than I had thus far recognized. What was holding me back? I know I must have been overheard on countless occasions saying, "I'll be happy when this or that happens in my life," most of which could be referenced to the scarcity of my thinking.

I soon came to understand that we would be happy only when we make the decision to be. Once we focus on all we have to be grateful for, the door to prosperity will open like a floodgate, pouring out the abundance we have been seeking. Those of us who say we will be happy when something happens have it backward. Rather, our dreams will be fulfilled when we choose to be happy. Life comes with challenges—some big, some small. The way we react to the smaller ones reveals us, and the way we respond to the bigger ones determines who we will become. All the challenges we face are truly opportunities to become better people. Sometimes it is extremely difficult to approach life's difficulties with a positive attitude. On the other hand, it is a great deal easier than living the life of someone who sees his or her self as a victim.

When my friends extended their invitation, I had yet to understand how to even begin to set my mind free. I grasped many principles from an intellectual perspective; however, much remained a mystery, and it is difficult to hit a target you fail to see. I acknowledged that there was likely a better way to approach life than the way I had been approaching it, but I could not see any other path than the one I had been on for such a long time. The problem with this path was that it was not taking me where I wanted to be, nor was I having much fun along the way. I knew I was missing something. I just could not seem to figure out what it was. All I was sure of was that some people had solved the so-called riddle and had subsequently learned how to get where they desired to be. I asked myself what it was they understood. I was failing to see my life as it could be. I recall questioning what would be possible in my life were I to be able to step outside of myself, outside of my problems, and see everything from an entirely different perspective. Would I recognize opportunities I had never recognized before? Could I be freed from the negative conditioning of my childhood, and were I to bury it once and for all, would I find peace?

The answer would be a resounding *yes*! I took my friends up on their generous offer. Four days can change a person's life. I gained more insight into what had been holding me back in those four days than I had in my thirty-five years. The experience could be likened to assembling a puzzle. Each of us has experienced many of life's critical lessons through the years, but typically we are missing a few that prevent us from seeing the whole picture. I was now free for the first time in my life. With childlike enthusiasm I set out to apply what I had learned. In the following days I wrote down five significant goals I wanted to accomplish — some required me to really stretch my faith as I never had before. Over the course of the next six months, I achieved every one. Yes, we can change, and we can change for the better!

Five years passed, when in the spring of 2000 I contracted with a company to develop its sales and marketing program. One of the employees approached me wanting to know how to achieve what he desired in life. In that training I outlined the formula I have utilized for more than a decade now, comprising what I refer to as "Life's Critical Elements to Creating Success."

These steps, when combined sequentially, will unlock the power of the universe. You may think I am joking with you. Do what I am about to suggest and judge for you.

1. You must first identify what you want. Do you really want it? Why do you want it? Does what you desire conflict with your values?

2. See yourself doing the very thing you want to do. Let your imagination take you away. Visualize your life the way you desire it to be, and do so frequently. Does it feel right to you? Is it what you have been meant to do? You will know!

3. Make your declaration to the universe and to someone you trust. Consider asking the person to hold you accountable for the *commitment* you have made. Your declaration should be stated in *I am*. Once you have committed yourself, be prepared because the universe will rise up to assist you. Believe me, Napoleon Hill knew what he was talking about.

4. Write it all down as it comes to you, and be detailed in describing all you desire. Whatever it may be, add it to your life's list of things to do. Prioritize it and weigh the costs. Are you willing to pay the price? When your answer is unequivocally yes, go for it!

5. Take massive and immediate action. There are physical laws at work here, and you are not going to end up where you desire to be while waiting for someone to knock your door down. You had better be pounding on theirs. This is a great time to seek the

help of others. Once you have demonstrated you have something exceptional to offer to the world, you can rest a while.

6. Opportunity will present itself. Do not worry about finding what you are looking for or if it will find you. *Have faith that the good you have asked for will be granted to you.* Be cautious in assessing your motives, and always investigate to make sure the opportunity is genuine. If for some reason you find you are not making progress, pray for guidance. Ask aloud and then be silent while you await the answers you seek; they will come. In the interim, release the outcome and move on to another task for a while.

7. Recognize opportunities as they present themselves. Prepare yourself so you know an opportunity when you encounter one. Seek outside council or the additional education you may need.

8. Master the "Five Steps of Influence." We will cover these in the coming pages. You are not going to get very far in life if you are not successful in influencing the decisions of those with whom you come into contact. Somebody out there has or possesses the means necessary for you to get what you want.

Well, there it is in black and white—a concise formula to creating the life you have dreamed of living, the ingredients a series of specific actions, which virtually assure your success.

Session 9 Summary

- Consider the impossible.
- Go for it!
- Command the elements by making your declaration.
- Life works when you ask the right questions.
- Have you been listening?
- See your life through the eyes of a child.
- Use the formula — there is no need to wait until all else fails.

Your Exercises for the Week

1. You must raise $100,000 within thirty days for a new business venture. How will you do it? Write down your answer before proceeding.

2. Now you must raise $100,000 within thirty days to provide an operation that will save the life of a loved one, perhaps yourself. How will you do it? Think creatively, and look for the unreasonable.

3. Which scenario above provided the greatest motivation? Did you take into account what you may have at one time consider impossible?

4. Now place the same level of importance on your dreams. What will you do to accomplish them? Write your answers down. I do not care how ridiculous they may appear at present.

5. Pay attention to the questions you have been asking, and make every effort possible to assure you are asking quality questions from this point forward.

Session Review

_____
_____
_____
_____
_____
_____
_____
_____
_____
_____
_____
_____
_____
_____
_____
_____
_____
_____
_____
_____
_____
_____
_____
_____
_____
_____
_____

SERVE OTHERS WELL

There are multiple ways we can give to others. We can give through serving, sharing knowledge, and by donating labor, time, or money. When we give, despite our penchant to believe we do not possess the means, we discover the empowerment that follows is far more enriching than the cost of the contribution we made. It comes down to the feelings derived from assisting another; we feel good about ourselves and as a result, we become empowered. We frequently receive more from giving than the recipient of our assistance. The more we give, the more we recognize we cannot give without receiving.

It Is Greater to Give Than to Receive

Perhaps you have seen the film *Pay it Forward*, starring Kevin Spacey, Helen Hunt, and Haley Joel Osment. It is a favorite of mine. The movie captures the essence of this principle as well as the joy we experience when living in accordance with the truth that it is greater to give than to receive. People who are fearful of giving are actually reaffirming their scarcity; they are afraid they do not have the means or ability to replace what they have given. Or they may just simply be selfish. Either way, the universe reflects the image of their actions. Those who are generous attract abundance, when what they put out comes back to them.

Givers gain; it is that simple. When we offer our resources without expectations, we plant a seed that will take root in others lives as well as our own. The root system eventually intertwines with the earth, holding the soil containing life's critical nutrients in place. The soil sustains life itself and promotes our stability even in the most inclement weather. The effects of one simple act of kindness can be witnessed for generations, possibly altering the course of history forever. Few among us have a clue as to just how powerful we are. What may at first appear to be no more than a small gesture of kindness can in fact change many lives. Read *The Greatest Salesman in the World,* by Og Mandino. You will find yourself inspired.

I have a dear friend I have known since childhood. She played a significant role in my life during my early years, and she is truly one of the most generous people I have ever met. I can recall having numerous conversations with her during the height of the Cold War when the possibility of a nuclear weapons conflict was looming like a dark cloud of terror overhead. If you are anywhere close to my age you will likely never forget this.

I remember sharing my concerns with my friend pertaining to the planet's poor environmental condition, the arms race, and what I perceived to be an inadequate response by the leadership of nations with respect to both. What was our generation going to be faced with? I certainly was not finding any comfort in the government's foreign policy or from the religious leaders of the time.

I had a conversation with a pastor, who attempted to comfort me by citing scripture that prophesied these things would be witnessed in the end of times. He pretty much instructed me not to be concerned. After all, why should I lose sleep over the possibility that some lunatic might unleash the horrors of hell upon all humanity? When I confronted him with our responsibility to prevent such a catastrophe, the pastor assured me there was nothing we could do about it. I could not believe my ears; his thinking was disturbingly irrational. I then truly understood for the first time the reason we were in this mess in the first place. Too many of us think we have no responsibility in determining the outcome of our existence. We do not appear to be able to take responsibility for our lives. We disregard the truth that we possess the free will to do what is necessary to turn the tide.

I do not wish to offend anyone. What I do intend to do is challenge the human race to get off their oversized complacent asses and contribute something constructive with regard to cleaning up the mess we have created. Quit waiting for someone else to do it for you. You and I have to recognize that we are the designated stewards of our lives, this planet and every breathtakingly beautiful living thing on it. We have been engineered to create, and it is time we begin creating heaven here on Earth.

The young woman I spoke of earlier not only shared the concerns of millions with respect to the plight of our world, she also possessed the determination to act upon those concerns. She would read for hours on every topic pertinent to the preservation of peace. She studied philosophy, physics, military strategy, books by world leaders, scientists, environmentalists, and the like. She read them in volumes, often into the wee hours of the night. More importantly, she possessed the intelligence to comprehend and retain the information she read. She began asking some very good questions, questions that would provide a formidable proposition to the leaders of the world. Ultimately this young woman accomplished one of the most amazing feats I have ever witnessed.

Serving Humanity

In 1981 this young woman proceeded to formulate a thirty-five point, multilateral, verifiable disarmament plan and soon thereafter submitted it to the attendees of a special meeting of the United Nations. Every delegate received a copy. Additionally, copies were forwarded to the governing bodies of all of the leading military nations, among them, the United States and former Soviet Union. The effort she put forth had been at her own expense. She had sought the financial support of a number of foundations and celebrities, and though many verbalized their support, none stepped forward to provide the financial assistance she so earnestly deserved. Eventually, members of the scientific community, some exceptional people in their own right, quietly acknowledged the brilliance of her work. By all accounts the plan was well received at the United Nations, and she waited optimistically for someone of great influence to seize the opportunity to end the Cold War.

Some years later President Ronald Reagan challenged Mikhail Gorbachev to tear down the Berlin Wall. This came to pass in 1990, and Gorbachev won the Nobel Peace Prize for his contributions to the peace process. What follows is an excerpt from the Norwegian Nobel Committee's letter announcing its recognition of Gorbachev, and is pertinent to the multilateral, verifiable disarmament plan drafted and submitted by this young woman to the United Nations eight years before:

"The Norwegian Nobel Committee has decided to award the 1990 Nobel Peace Prize to Mikhail Sergeyevich Gorbachev, president of the Soviet Union, for his leading role in the peace process which today characterizes important parts of the international community.

During the last few years, dramatic changes have taken place in the relationship between the East and West. Confrontation has been replaced by negotiations. Old European nation states have regained their freedom. The arms race is slowing down, and we see a definite and active process in the direction of arms control and disarmament. Several regional conflicts have been solved or have at least come closer to a solution. The U.N. is beginning to play the role which was originally planned for it in an international community governed by law.

These historic changes spring from several factors, but in 1990 the Nobel Committee wants to honor Mikhail Gorbachev for his many and decisive contributions. The greater openness he has brought about in Soviet society has also helped promote international trust.

In the opinion of the Committee, this peace process, which Gorbachev has contributed so significantly to, opens up new possibilities for the world community to solve its pressing problems across ideological, religious, historical, and cultural dividing lines." [1]

Gorbachev's plan was published in the *New York Times,* and two great nations that had been teetering on the brink of total annihilation for more than forty years had finally relaxed their posture. The world, no doubt, was far better off than before. With respect to this young woman and Gorbachev, though they had never met, their plans shared a common and rather remarkable resemblance. Perhaps it was merely coincidence, though I doubt it. Please do not misinterpret me. I am in no way challenging the authenticity of Mr. Gorbachev's work. However, I have often wondered whether her submission to the United Nations and to the U.S. offices of the Soviet Embassy found its way to the Soviet leader, inspiring him to take action.

Whatever moved Gorbachev to do what he did, my friend was thrilled someone as strategically postured in the world's political community as he, had acknowledged the severity of the threat posed by the nuclear arms race and made the choice to do something about it. Finally, there was someone who proposed that an alternative strategy to Mutual Assured Destruction (MAD) existed; one that incorporated intelligence and signified the human race was moving beyond insanity. Though (MAD) still remains the primary deterrent, at least the clock

---

[1] Oslo, October 15, 1990.

has been turned back, and we do not appear to be gazing into the abyss as we were for the better part of the last century. Though this woman was never formally recognized for her service to humanity as she should have been, she never expressed her disappointment. She instead breathed a sigh of relief, grateful the world was now a safer place for all.

We often measure success monetarily, but monetary success can at times be the least important of our accomplishments. Just ask parents who have found themselves alienated from their child, or watched as their child headed down a destructive path. This can leave a parent wondering whether they should have given their child more attention and fewer toys. Our success may demand we remove profit from the equation entirely. We may find that success requires us to draw upon all of our resources until we have been relieved not only of our money, time, and energy, but also our patience. When pursuing our dreams, we may discover it is best for us to acquiesce to a will greater than our own.

Remember, there are many ways we can serve those we come into contact with. We can begin by just listening to others. Often this is the only thing they are seeking—someone who will listen and empathize with their situation. A business can greatly increase customer loyalty by insuring their employees listen to their customers. The profit a company may initially experience through budget cuts (requiring customer service training be eliminated) will quickly vanish in the resulting loss of customers; it is not enough to simply keep a customer satisfied. When you want a customer to go to work for you promoting your business, your business had better see to it that your customer is more than satisfied. The customer had better be elated.

Consumers do not talk about performance that meets their expectations; however, they *do* talk about performance that exceeds their expectations. It makes no sense for a business to invest vast sums of money into advertising while failing to invest in customer-service training. This scenario is as ludicrous as individuals accumulating financial wealth without creating friends with whom to share their good fortune.

I had an experience a few years back that made a frustrating event far more pleasant than it otherwise would have been. A pipe broke in the wall of my home office, and water flooded the room. This room was furnished with modular systems typically found in a commercial office setting. Upon discovering the saturated carpet, I thought of all the work it would entail to disassemble the modular furniture. Though it would have been easy to dwell on the work that lay ahead, I knew this would leave me even more aggravated. So instead, I focused on our good fortune: the whole basement hadn't flooded, just the office. Although we may gain some temporary relief from venting, it really does not do much good to complain. We might as well get to work and resolve the problem as quickly as possible...which is what we did.

My wife and I went to work dismantling and relocating the furniture. We then extracted gallons of water from the carpet. I cruised down to the local equipment-rental franchise to acquire the commercial carpet dryer we needed. First, however, we made sure the source of the leak had been contained. We called our plumber and he showed up as promised the following morning. Upon completing his work, he examined the damage from the flooding. Empathetic to our misfortune, he responded by reducing his normal fees by fifty percent. This is the kind of service that will promote customer loyalty, wouldn't you agree? Things were already looking a little brighter.

Another day passed before the carpet had completely dried. Upon returning the rented equipment, I had the good fortune of being greeted by the store manager. He asked how things had gone. I told him the blower had done what we needed and thanked him for asking. He replied, "Oh, no problem at all. I just know when someone rents one of these babies it usually means they have their work cut out for them. Let's see here; it looks like you had this machine for two days. Tell you what; I am only going to charge you for one!"

Wow, I thought to myself, *that's twice now that two different people have offered to reduce their fees by 50 percent*—all because they empathized with our burden. In my opinion, what is so great about experiences like these is that they reinforce our faith in humanity. It is amazingly refreshing—like being presented with a gift of kindness, generosity, and the feeling that you are not alone. This is among the greatest gifts anyone can present to another. When was the last time someone offered to go out of their way for you, and how did it make you feel? Imagine what you could do to positively affect the lives of someone you may not even know. A simple act of kindness can reverberate in the hearts and minds of the recipient for a lifetime.

All of us, with the anger, fear, and hostility we witness daily, could benefit a great deal by simply being more courteous to one another. We can begin with rudimentary acts of kindness — being the first to greet the stranger at the store, welcoming a new neighbor to the community, or assisting someone in need. Little acts of kindness make all the difference in how we perceive our world and those within it.

Remember what I shared about the obstacles we face? There is always something to be gained when we approach them with a positive attitude. As for the store manager, I found out his franchise was among the top-performing locations in the western United States. It had not been that way prior to his arrival the previous spring. I told him it was apparent why he had made such progress in an exceptionally short period of time, and that he could be assured I would promote his business throughout the community.

This is a fine example of two businessmen who appreciated what it means to show compassion for the predicament of another. Both chose the path of service rather than seizing the opportunity to maximize their profit. Be assured both of these gentlemen will continue to profit from their kindness. Certainly this event was both aggravating and time consuming, and yet the good will these men demonstrated offered some welcomed compensation for the interruption to our lives. It is always nice to be reminded we are not alone in our struggles. The encouragement that can be gained in witnessing simple acts of kindness is like an updraft lifting us to new heights of hope and aspiration.

We are mistaken to await the invitation of others to lead. Leadership should be born of our own initiative. Be quick to give, and ask for nothing more of your benefactors than to pass on your good will to another so the cycle may be perpetuated. When the human race truly comprehends the relevance of this principle and when it becomes the rule rather than the exception, I expect life here on Earth will mirror the heavens.

Help!

When I struggle with an issue, or feel depressed and isolated, I find the cure to what ails me when I focus on the needs of others. When I support others, I become strengthened. When I accept support from another without embarrassment, I am a better person. You and I are part of the whole; therefore we remain incomplete when we remain segregated from the love and encouragement of others.

When you truly love yourself, you will permit yourself to give as you have never given before. You will hunger for the feeling you derive from your philanthropic acts. There is no substitution—nothing compares to what you will experience. You will find yourself truly becoming more empowered when you give to another. I challenge you to put this to the test. You will not be sorry you did. Begin now and give often.

In turn, *remember to ask for help* when you really need it. I wish I had asked for help when I was struggling to provide for my mother and me as a teenager. I wish I had possessed the humility and insight to seek the assistance of my counselors at school as well as the guidance of friends and family, which may have made all difference. I was embarrassed and too proud to disclose my circumstances. I would have just as soon died as to speak of my struggles. I chose instead to hide my condition from those who could have assisted me, and consequently I paid a dear price for my choice in the years to follow. Do not be afraid to ask for assistance. You may have to ask more than one person and you may have to ask more than once. Keep asking until you find the assistance and answers you require.

The Traits which Drive Us

Understanding the personality traits which drive us will make your life easier. As we live and conduct business, we most likely find ourselves interacting with others. Some may choose to limit their contact with other people; others may seem unable to surround themselves with enough people. Which are you? We all posses distinguishing traits. The common characteristics we share can be defined and categorized into four quadrants. You will benefit in being able to quickly identify the predominant traits of those with whom you come in contact. This will permit you to communicate more effectively, and your ability to do so will play a critical role in your success.

Our individual characteristics permit us to categorize the generalities of the human personality. Over the years many formulas have been developed, providing a better understanding of the various personalities. It serves us well to understand how people perceive their world and those within it. After all, whatever you want to obtain, someone else likely holds the key to your acquiring it. This is true for almost everything! For brevity's sake, I will only address one of the formulas. Naturally, it is the one I have found to be the most effective in permitting individuals to quickly determine the communication style of others.

The personality traits of most people can be reduced to four primary quadrants: (1) the controlling personality, (2) the promoting personality, (3) the analytical personality, and (4) the supportive personality. One of these personality styles is predominate in almost every person. Still, these characteristics typically overlap with the other quadrants. We also frequently find that another quadrant would have better defined our behavior as children than the one we identify with as adults. Our original style could best be described as our *natural* style, rather than the *adaptive* style defining us today. Some of us may find our style has remained the same.

The characteristics described in the following pages determine how we perceive and approach the world around us. As you progress through this session you will begin to identify the personality traits of others. Doing so will enable you to communicate with individuals far more effectively than before.

The Controller: Frequently referred to as a *driver*, the Controller is readily distinguished by their decisiveness. Often viewed as opinionated and demanding, they like things their way. They respond favorably to questions beginning with "What." Controllers generally dislike wasting time, listening to excessive talkers, or associating with those who attempt to make their decisions for them. They would prefer it if you would "cut to the chase" and "get to the bottom line." They respond to pressure by taking the lead or becoming increasingly controlling. They like being in charge and prefer to be identified with results. They must be allowed to compete, and they love to win. They typically experience greater personal growth in situations requiring the cooperation of others. They prefer to save time, completing tasks now rather than later. Efficiency ranks highest with them. To lead them effectively, it is best to allow them the freedom to do things their way.

The Promoter: Frequently referred to as an *expressive*, the Promoter tends to be excitable, outgoing, and enthusiastic, often being recognized as the life of the party. These individuals love to have fun. They respond favorably to "Who" questions. They dislike boring explanations, so avoid tying them down with too many detail or facts (or you will quickly lose their attention). They react to pressure by selling their ideas or becoming increasingly persuasive. Inclined to be argumentative, they respond well to others who share their enthusiasm. They feel comfortable with displays of emotion. They like to be measured by the applause they receive — recognition is important to them. They must be provided the opportunity to advance quickly. They respond well to a challenge. They improve with structure and recognition for their accomplishments. Promoters prefer to minimize their effort while relying on their intuition or instincts to lead them. To lead them effectively, inspire them to achieve bigger and better results.

The Analytical: Continually seeking information, the Analytical thrives on data, and asks a great deal of questions. They respond favorably to questions beginning with "How." Generally methodical in the way they approach life, they lose confidence in others unless they are shown patience. They dislike being caught unprepared, finding it embarrassing when they do not have an answer. They hate to make mistakes, and they like to save face. They generally respond to pressure by seeking more information. They receive others well when provided with detailed and accurate information. They prefer to be measured by, or recognized for, their activity and production. Let the Analytical make decisions at their own pace, and avoid pressuring them. They improve by focusing on their relationships and communications skills. They respond well to leadership providing them a structured environment.

The Amiable: The Amiable or *supportive* individual loves positive attention. Amiable people like to be recognized as helpful, warm, and friendly. They respond favorably to questions beginning with "Why." They dislike rejection or people who demonstrate an impersonal, uncaring, or unfeeling attitude toward others. When pressured, they become silent, withdrawn, or introspective. It is imperative to treat the Amiable with the care and support they deserve. They like to be measured by their ability to develop meaningful relationships. They must be allowed to relax and socialize. Let them build the relationships they seek. They will improve when provided structure with clearly defined goals and systems in place. Above all, an effective leader must remember and respect the value the Amiable places on relationships.

The Controller, the Promoter, the Analytical and the Amiable—these are the foremost personality traits found among people. You likely identified the predominant personality of those you are acquainted with—yourself included. Now you are prepared to examine the role this plays in your personal interaction with others.

Let us begin by drawing a matrix (this will permit us to review how each of these personalities respond when interacting with another). Start by drawing a straight, six-inch, vertical line in the middle of a blank sheet of paper. Then draw a horizontal line of equal length with the two lines intersecting at their middle. You should have a large plus sign. Now write the words Controller/Driver in the upper left quadrant of your diagram, the word Analytical in the upper right quadrant, the words Promoter/Expressive in the bottom left, and Amiable/Supportive in the lower right. You have initiated your matrix.

As you study the matrix, notice the diagonal opposite of the Controlling personality is the Supportive personality. The diagonal opposite of the Analytical personality is the Promoting personality. The horizontal and vertical alignments tend to share more in common characteristically than the diagonal.

If you have identified the Supportive personality as the one best describing you, you are more likely to share the characteristics of either the Analytical or the Promoting personalities. For example, you may be a Supportive Analytical. The Supportive defines the predominant characteristics in your personality, while the Analytical personality possesses many characteristics you relate to. Naturally, you may identify from time to time with some traits in all four quadrants, but he majority of people always recognize specific traits within a particular personality type as best describing their behavior.

We are all capable of adapting our style as necessary, though this is not to say we adjust as we should. Our successful adaptation often requires a great deal of self-discipline; however, the Supportive individual, for example, adopts many of the Controlling personality traits when acting in a managerial capacity. At times this is an absolute necessity to the survival of the Supportive individual in a business setting.

Speaking in generalities, the Controlling personality often has a low tolerance for the diametrically opposed Supportive personality and vice versa. The same is true for the Analytical and Promoting personalities. The Controller places more emphasis on results than on relationships, whereas the Supporter places relationships above all else. The Controller tends to believe theirs is the only way. The Supporter is likely to be considerably more flexible in their approach to finding a solution and traditionally demonstrates greater patience for the feelings of others. Supporters tend to mistrust Controllers, seeing them as self-serving and generally demonstrating little concern for the impact of their behavior.

Supporters often credit Controllers for their ability to get things done and generally describe them as dynamic, tenacious, and typically possessing strong leadership skills. Supporters may have reservations regarding the Controllers' lack of concern for the well-being of others when they are out to accomplish a given task. In contrast, Controllers may see Supporters as weak and indecisive, often yielding to popular opinion in order to keep everyone happy. On the other hand, Controllers recognize the value of aligning themselves in work and in life with Supporters, the two are often found as partners in business and marriage. This is likely because the human personality consciously or unconsciously desires the strengths that may be derived from another. Personalities seek their compliment. Couples who have spent a great deal of time together grow ever closer in mirroring the traits of the other. The Supporter likely becomes bolder, and the Controller more patient.

Promoters are often credited for their enthusiasm and social skills, while the Analytical would prefer to limit their social interaction in favor of a project. They frequently perceive enthusiastic people as flighty and undependable. Analytical personalities seek information, often down to the smallest detail, while the Promoters attention is lost with too much detail. Like the Controller, the Promoter prefers conciseness.

Promoters place a great deal of trust in their intuition, while the Analytical prefers facts, seeking detailed information when it comes to making decisions. Promoters become agitated with the time it may require for an Analytical to make a decision, and their patience typically wanes long before the Analytical is prepared to act. It serves Promoters to be patient with the Analytical in their quest for additional information when doing business because they can be a great source of referrals. The Analytical opinion inspires confidence. Known for their exhaustive research, they are unlikely to represent anything for other than what it is. Additionally, the Analytical is exceptionally loyal to those who demonstrate a willingness to accommodate their voracious need for detailed information.

The Analytical may express their concern with regard to the overzealous and haphazard behavior they interpret to be characteristic of the Promoter. The Analytical personality is frequently skeptical of those who make decisions based on their so-called intuitiveness. The Analytical will typically acknowledge the promoters' exceptional social skills, further accrediting them with their enthusiastic and optimistic approach to life. Promoters generally demonstrate their appreciation for the thoroughness with which the Analytical approaches tasks. Promoters often express they could have completed several tasks in the time it takes an Analytical to accomplish just one. The Analytical openly points out the Promoters' tendency to make a multitude of mistakes, while deeming the quality of their performance as substandard. There is little doubt in the Analytical mind that the Promoter would be far better off investing the required time and energy to complete a thorough investigation of the facts before proceeding.

The Controlling and Analytical personalities are traditionally formal by nature, whereas the Promoting and Supportive personalities are, as a rule, informal. The Controller and Promoter lean heavily toward being dominant, while the Analytical and Supporter are typically easygoing, with a flow-with personality. A quick review of the matrix reveals the Controller is a "formal dominant," and the Supporter is an "informal flow-with." All four quadrants can be credited with possessing their own unique strengths, and it would be appropriate to point out that our greatest strengths may also be recognized as our greatest weaknesses. When you apply theses insights, you will communicate more effectively. Do not be surprised to discover yourself expressing your thoughts in a manner others can more readily relate to. With observation and practice you should find your family, friends, and even complete strangers increasingly cooperative when seeking their support.

Success is seldom a result of our haphazard behavior, and it is almost impossible to perpetuate a winning streak in the absence of a clearly defined plan. Just as there is a genetic formula for every living thing, there is a formula for living the life of your dreams. The sequential process outlined is the formula I speak of, and it will provide the natural continuity required to bring your reality into alignment with your dreams. This process, as you have by now undoubtedly recognized, is comprised of sound, time-proven principles.

You can now consciously emulate the process, perfecting your performance as you go. A life of fulfillment is a life lived with intent and the acceptance of the responsibility that *we* play the most critical role in what we achieve. I again encourage you to quit reacting to life and instead take the actions necessary to create the life you desire.

"How is it we Americans give more attention to designing the interior of our homes and more thought to the car we choose to purchase than we do to crafting a plan for our lives?" —Mark A. Maxon

Session 10 Summary
- It is greater to give than to receive.
- We can serve in many ways.
- Ask for help.
- Mirror others' personality types.

Your Exercises for the Week
1. Write a list of the different ways you are currently serving others.
2. Analyze the type of service you have been rendering.
3. Who can you serve this week?
4. Note the areas on your things-to-do list for which you could ask assistance.
5. Complete the personality matrix, noting your personality as well as the personalities of those with whom you interact often.

6. Write down some ideas as to how you can communicate more effectively with these individuals.
7. Continue using your things-to-do list on a daily basis.

Session Review

_____
_____
_____
_____
_____
_____
_____
_____
_____
_____
_____
_____
_____
_____
_____
_____
_____
_____
_____
_____
_____
_____
_____
_____

SESSION 11
THE FIVE STEPS OF EFFECTIVE INFLUENCE

Welcome to Session 11 with your personal coach. Whatever you aspire to achieve, it will at some point likely require the cooperation of another. To gain the support you seek, understand that person's personality style and make use of the formula I refer to as the Five Steps of Effective Influence. Most of us desire, or are required, to periodically influence those we come into contact with. Your ability to adequately influence individuals to act in a manner benefiting them will be reflected in the results you achieve.

Relatively young corporations have surpassed well-established industry giants because of their upper management's ability to influence others. Nations have been built and governments overthrown as a direct result of one individual's power to persuade the people. Wars have been avoided and wars have been waged for the same reason. Imagine what your life would look like were you to master the art of influencing others. Your potential would be unlimited. Now, before you become carried away with your thoughts of manipulating others, understand you will be more successful in accomplishing what you desire by assisting others in achieving their aspirations. Remember to make the needs and desires of others as important as your own, and everyone will win. When others associate you with positive results, you will be welcome in any relationship, social setting, or business environment. Mastering the steps of effective influence will equip you to lead people as never before.

The Five Steps of Effective Influence

1. Introduction: Every good idea, product, or service warrants a worthy introduction. The quality of your introduction sets the tone for how you are perceived, and to what degree others will cooperate with you. In the introduction you must catch the attention of your listener, and establish the trust that will permit you to identify the listener's interests, needs, and desires. Your introduction must contain an *interest-creating remark* or *captivating statement* to catch the listener's undivided attention. We have little time to spark the interest of another. Most individuals have a relatively short attention span; they are preoccupied with other issues demanding their concentration or providing a distraction. Those specializing in advertising understand the importance of quickly gaining the attention of their audience.

The key to fashioning an effective *interest-creating remark* is to immediately focus on the benefits of your product, service or idea. Structure your introduction with words that paint a vivid picture of what you desire the targeted market to visualize. The visual image of their success will fuel their emotional attachment to the outcome. Once emotionally involved, an individual who may have otherwise been uninterested now desires to know more. The fact is everyone wants to know what is in it for them; they want to know how they will benefit.

Without explanation, the features of a product or service provide little correlation to the benefit they provide. We make the mistake of assuming someone will associate the feature with the benefit. To correlate is the same as to show a relationship, and this is exactly what you want to do—draw a picture of how others will benefit from whatever you are selling, whether it is an idea, product, service, or yourself.

Everyone is better served when we move directly to the payoff. Get to the point quickly, explaining how one can gain from investing the time to evaluate the merit of what you are offering. Emphasize what is in it for them, while keeping your initial introduction concise. Detailed information will be covered at the appropriate time. It is extremely important you understand their position before you elaborate; this is accomplished through what I refer to as the discovery process.

The sole purpose of your introduction is to establish the value others will receive by responding to your discovery. The sale herein is in gaining another to allow you access to information they may consider personal or perhaps highly confidential. As I explain to my clients in the sales industry, the purpose of the introduction is to convey, or sell, the value of the discovery, which lays the foundation for the integrity of the sale. It would be a grave mistake to attempt to sell or influence another without first understanding the person's mindset, needs, and desires.

Remember, the purpose of the introduction and the *interest creating remark* is to gain the attention of the desired audience in order to establish the value of the discovery, nothing more. Once you have sparked their curiosity, you will have little problem gaining their cooperation.

There are times we might be guilty of interrupting the individual we seek to serve. This is undoubtedly the reason many people are apprehensive about approaching someone in the first place, despite the value of what they are offering. When you do have something exceptional to offer others, you must not hesitate to let them know. They deserve the opportunity to decide for themselves if it will benefit them. It is not always easy to gain an audience with someone, especially when they are apprehensive about being sold something they do not want or need. None of us likes to be sold; however, we do appreciate being served. Sometimes it is necessary for you to interrupt another during their busy day in order to do so. When people recognize the value you have to offer, the interruption will be welcome.

The overall success you will experience in commanding the attention of others will have everything to do with how creative you are. Retaining interest after you have interrupted someone is the key to garnering the support needed to learn what must be known in order to gain an invitation to serve the person.

2. Discovery: The most important trait we can nurture is our propensity to ask quality questions and to listen attentively to the response of others. Follow the systematic approach I have outlined for you and you will become proficient in identifying the needs and desires of others; your job then is to serve them accordingly. I will once again emphasize the most important trait we can nurture within ourselves is our adeptness to ask quality questions and our willingness to listen attentively to others. Therein lies the key to success.

The discovery consists of a series of questions which permit you to assess the personality type, needs, desires, and general attitude of those with whom you interact. Among the most important questions you will ask will be queries allowing you to determine who will make the final decision with respect to whatever you will be proposing. A thorough discovery will provide the insight required to posture your recommendations in a manner demonstrating your genuine desire to serve others interests. When asking the right questions, you will be perceived as knowledgeable, and your recommendations will be welcomed. An effective discovery provides the insight necessary to present your recommendations in such a way that others will be receptive.

A quality discovery is comprised of questions demonstrating a strong understanding of the needs and desires of the individuals you seek to serve. First, assess the strengths and weaknesses of your competition. Second, determine what your previous customer's most prevalent concerns were when you first approached them for their business. Make sure your discovery consists of questions that will extract any similar concerns your prospective customer may have as early as possible. It is better that you attention is drawn to such concerns early on rather than having them revealed when attempting to call your customer to action. Having accomplished this, you will be prepared to address concerns at the appropriate time.

Inquire if the customer is familiar with the product or service you are representing, and ask what their feelings may be toward it. Have they had a previous experience with something similar? Was it a positive experience? What could your competitor have improved upon? Avoid anything that remotely resembles an attempt to sell your idea, product, or service at this time. This is the time to learn, so ask questions that are relevant to unveiling the needs and desires of the individual you are addressing. Pay close attention to the individual's response. Observe their body language and breathing, and listen as much to what is not being said as to what is being said. We can often learn a great deal about the real attitude someone may have with us or our offering by recognizing the person's failure to interact.

I remember an experience I once had with a gentleman when visiting his office. I had failed in persuading him to participate in an honest exchange. He was holding back, and it would have been useless for me to attempt to proceed without his interest. When people sense something is not as it should be, they often ignore their instincts in fear that should they speak up, the other party may take offense. They might as well thank them for their time and excuse themselves. Having learned this the hard way, I decided to speak up; politely commenting that it was apparent I had lost his interest. I apologized for failing to convey the value that would be gained through his participation. He in turn apologized and shared his reasons for his disinterest. With this, he revealed the key to capturing his undivided attention...within the hour he became my client.

There was a time I would have failed to read this man. I would have avoided such a direct confrontation, fearful of losing his business. What is important to understand is that I never had his business in the first place, and I was certainly not going to earn it by pretending all was fine. As long as I remained politely in my place, he would have remained politely quiet, never disclosing his skepticism towards my industry. This all changed after I provided him with an incentive to be honest with me.

Together we got down to the heart of what was preventing him from stepping forward and doing what was in his best interest—that is what I call success. This individual and I went beyond superficiality and became real with one another. I am convinced this is what people seek above all else—people who are not afraid to be real with us. To achieve what you desire, be real with others first!

Another example of the power in the discovery process involved a potential account I called upon in the dental industry many years ago. This particular practice had two offices. I met with the administrative manager of one of the offices and conducted the standard discovery. We both concluded my service would provide the solutions the practice had been seeking. During the discovery, however, I learned this young woman was not the decision-maker for the practice. Having gained her confidence, she insisted on calling her supervisor, recommending she meet with me as soon as her schedule would permit.

Two weeks later I met the actual decision-maker, and it was not the supervisor as had been indicated to me. Upon arriving at the practice, I introduced myself to Kathy (the supervisor) and stated the purpose of my visit. I quickly summarized the benefits (not the features) our services would provide to the practice. Kathy was interested. I recommended we review the discovery from my previous meeting to make sure all parties agreed with the information. We completed the discovery, concluding the original findings paralleled her own. Kathy stated she was responsible for deciding whether the practice would implement our services.

Confident Kathy would be receptive to my recommendation, I proceeded to review the features and benefits our services would provide. She loved the program. It was only then I learned she would have to interrupt the doctor for authorization. I realized Kathy did not have the decision-making power she had indicated. In all probability, the doctor would be responsible for making the final decision. This presented a small problem because the Doctor had no concept of the value his practice would receive for the money Kathy was about to request. I would have to meet with the doctor, just as I had met with both the office manager and supervisor. This did not present an obstacle for me, but it could possibly conflict with his schedule, and I would be forced to return at a later date. I am not much for wasting time, and I hate to put off to tomorrow what could be completed today. I prepared myself to gain an audience with the doctor then and there.

Kathy returned to report that the doctor was not interested at this time. I informed her I was not surprised under the circumstances. Without having reviewed the information, as she had, the doctor had no idea as to the value our services would provide the practice. I told Kathy I appreciated the doctor's position and asked her once again whether she agreed my services would provide a substantial benefit to the practice. She assured me the practice would save a great deal of time and money, and that the doctor's patients would be better served by implementing the program. Then I asked Kathy if she would agree the doctor deserved the courtesy of reviewing the benefits as she had so he could make an educated decision. Furthermore, I emphasized it would be a shame not to implement a program offering so many benefits simply because the doctor had not been presented the information. Kathy agreed and asked if I would give her a minute to approach the doctor once again. She returned momentarily, only to state that the doctor had a luncheon appointment immediately following the patient he was currently treating.

Some of you may think my response was a bit bold; nonetheless, I maintain a busy schedule and consider my time to be as valuable as anyone's. I had completed my due diligence and invested a great deal of time, so I made what I consider to be a reasonable request for a few minutes of the doctor's time. My intent was simply to quantify the doctor's level of interest and schedule my return accordingly. It had also been my experience that when a physician invested a few brief minutes to review the findings of his office manager, he would likely recognize the benefits of our services and enlist our expertise without further delay. I was determined to give it my all, right then!

Stating to Kathy what I have just shared with you, I asked if she would inform the doctor that I would be happy to schedule my return at a time more convenient for everyone. I simply wanted to introduce myself to him personally, present him an outline of our findings, and ask two or three questions that would determine if it would be in our mutual interest to meet again. I asked Kathy to further inform the doctor that the vice president of the company personally traveled a considerable distance to serve his practice, and it was seldom he would have the opportunity to speak with the horse's mouth. I emphasized I had rarely been associated with the other end of the animal. We laughed just long enough to alleviate any tension, and Kathy agreed it was worth one last effort. She returned moments later, informing me the doctor was willing to meet for a few minutes.

Upon entering the room, the doctor extended his hand, welcoming me. I thanked him, we reviewed the highlights of my recommendation, and my five minutes were up. I asked him if he concurred with Kathy's findings. He did. I then told him I would be happy to return. Instead, he asked if I would be willing to wait a few minutes so that we could complete our business, permitting Kathy to implement the program immediately. Incidentally, the doctor doubled the size of Kathy's order, authorizing a check for twice the original sum she had requested. Go figure! The doctor again offered his hand in gratitude for my time and persistence, and to my amazement apologized for having made it so difficult for me to meet with him.

I share this story for a number of reasons. First, I hope you believe as much in the value of what you have to offer as I do. If you do not, I recommend you reevaluate your position, provided you desire to rise to the top of your field. Second, you better value your time as well as the time of others. Last and perhaps most importantly, I hope you recognize how the discovery made it possible for me to serve the Doctor's practice. Lacking the knowledge I gained from the discovery, would have made it impossible for me to accomplish what I did.

Without question, knowledge is power. Knowledge empowers us so that we may serve often and well. Prior to making your recommendation to another, make sure you are well informed and in possession of the facts pertinent to serving the best interests of everyone involved. You will find your preparedness breeds confidence, and in your confidence you possess the conviction necessary to garner the attention of those you seek to serve. This is why the discovery should always precede your recommendation. None of us have the right to make a recommendation to another without first understanding their needs and desires. Furthermore, we should never do business with anyone without being confident that what we offer will benefit them. Always make sure you serve the interest of others as you would serve yourself.

3. Recommendation: The recommendation is the process of introducing your idea, product, or solution based on the information derived from the discovery process. You now possess the necessary information to focus on what is pertinent to the needs and interests of the individual or group to whom you are about to make a recommendation. You should be aware of the possible concerns and objections you may encounter, and be prepared to address them before they present a serious obstacle to completing the transaction.

When covering a specific feature, you now know the best way to relate its benefits in terms that your client will identify and appreciate. This is once again the appropriate time to use the power of pictorial communication, creating a clear picture of the positive outcome implements your product, service, or idea. Walk the client through the most relevant scenarios one by one.

I recall a former client who was a building contractor. I will call him Stan. When we met, Stan's sales ratios were less than satisfactory. He was successful in acquiring referrals from his existing customers—a sign of his dependability and superior service; however, Stan was not exceptionally proficient in converting his bids into income-generating relationships. Stan desired to change this.

As always, I conducted a discovery to determine what he was or was not doing to account for his unsatisfactory performance. I wanted to understand how he approached his introduction, discovery, recommendation, and so forth. It quickly became apparent Stan was a likable fellow who took great pride in providing quality craftsmanship. After finding out he was competitively priced, I asked him how he presented bids. He said first he reviewed the pending project with the prospective customer. The job might consist of a kitchen remodel, home addition, basement completion, or some other project. He would then return to the office, prepare his estimate, and present it to the prospect via fax, e-mail, parcel post, or personal delivery. I suggested he adjust his presentation, making sure to personally review his bids with all parties involved in making the decision to enlist his services. I told him this change would likely increase sales dramatically. I emphasized that an estimate worth preparing certainly justified his returning to present it in a manner suiting his professional standards.

In the following weeks Stan presented all of his estimates in person, making certain each decision-maker was present so he could review the details, ensuring his recommendations were to their satisfaction. This additionally provided Stan the opportunity to readdress the needs and desires of the prospect, assessing any changes necessary. He was now be in a position to walk through each step, drawing on the prospect's imagination to create a detailed picture of what the project would look like at completion. This presentation also permitted Stan to observe how enthusiastic the prospect was about moving forward. Stan was now in a position to review any other estimates his prospect might have received.

I explained to Stan when offering your customer the opportunity to draw upon your expertise—sincerely prepared to surrender your business to a competitor who may be offering a superior product or a comparable product at a lower price—you will typically gain more business than you will lose. At times you will find yourself turning business away because you are unable to accommodate the demand for your services. It all comes back around to the laws governing scarcity and abundance.

Stan asked me how to go about suggesting to a prospective customer that he assist them in reviewing a competitor's bid. I told him to simply let the prospect know he had come to realize that "what goes around comes around—everyone wins, particularly the customer." After all, Stan might recognize something another contractor overlooked, or he might discover something he had failed to consider. Most importantly, he could assure the prospect received the quality materials and craftsmanship they deserved. Now able to point out the superiority of the materials he had selected for the project, Stan was in a position to elaborate on the attention he liked to give to every detail, resulting in the added value of his craftsmanship. Stan was now able to quickly make discretionary adjustments in his estimates that would win the contract while in the company of his new customer.

When you make a recommendation, determine the prospect's response before moving on. I refer to this as the agreement process. Old-school sales training calls this the tie-down. I do not like what this implies. I am not interested in tying my customers down, up, or anything of the sort. I am interested in delivering what my customer needs and desires, making sure before we move forward on any project, we agree on what is to be accomplished. This typically results in a satisfied customer and a healthy relationship.

Stan was now in the position to address and overcome any concerns, schedule the job, and collect a deposit before being on his way. Stan committed to follow my recommendations and agreed if an estimate was worth preparing, it was worth reviewing with his prospects. In the following weeks, he wrote more business than he had in the previous six months. He was pretty excited with the results.

Subtle adjustments in the way we approach life and business make all the difference in the results we experience. The little things we do, or fail to do, either provide for or deprive us of our dreams. Stan had been skipping steps he deemed superfluous. By simply adjusting his course he easily arrived at his desired destination. What steps have you been skipping?

Review the recommendation process, and remember to introduce your recommendations with conviction. Others will likely place little value on your opinion when you fail to recognize its worth yourself. Always assure other parties the ultimate decision is theirs, and that your objective is to work together to achieve what is deemed to be in their best interest. When others are convinced you have their best interest at heart, they will be more forgiving when they find themselves in disagreement with you or your recommendations.

As you cover the features and benefits, ask prospects what they think. Do not be afraid to request elaboration. They may touch on things you have failed to, and you will learn what they are thinking. This typically promotes the success of everyone involved. You want to know others are paying attention to what you are saying and you can be assured they feel the same. Paying close attention to and honoring the view of others will likely promote a favorable exchange.

During your recommendation or presentation, ask if anyone has a question or concern. If so, refer to the instructions provided in the fifth step below: Isolating and Addressing Concerns. Continue the process I outlined until you have reviewed all which is pertinent to your recommendation. Then proceed to the next step.

4. Call to Action: It is now time to bring your exchange to a conclusion. Many of us struggle when it comes to requesting another take action, even when the evidence indicates that doing so is in the best interest of all parties. Ask whether your proposal meets the prospect's criteria. If it does, ask the prospect to take action in accordance with your recommendations. You will likely want to have an incentive in place for them to move forward in a timely manner.

When you follow the process as outlined, Introduction to Discovery, Discovery to Recommendation, and utilize the *agreement questions* referenced earlier, you should know what the prospect's response will be. Nevertheless, the questions must be asked. There is no reason to be intimidated by the possibility that the prospect may disagree or decline to do business at this time. Be silent and wait for a response. No matter how uncomfortable you may find the silence to be, you must not be the first to speak. Instead, you must give the prospect time to respond, and then listen thoughtfully to the response.

When a prospect commits to take action immediately, accept your success graciously, congratulate them on their decision, and express your delight at the alliance established. Thank the client for their business, reminding them that you are grateful for the opportunity to serve. On the other hand, should the prospect decline your offer, do not be disappointed. Instead, put forth the effort to understand the person's reasoning. Align yourself with them by voicing your appreciation for their position. Let them know you are at a disadvantage because you fail to understand how they arrived at their decision.

Here is an example of how you might address someone who wants time to think their decision through.

"Mark, I value your position. My experience has been that when someone tells me they need to think it over, it generally indicates one of two things. They have some questions remaining unanswered, or they are considering how to move forward financially; which applies to you?"

Wait for a response. You will find that most of the time the person will tell you exactly what is preventing them from moving forward. Whatever the reason, isolate and address their concerns.

5. Isolate and Address Concerns: All circumstances considered, it is perfectly natural for people to be concerned about making the best possible decision to serve their interests. I was raised in a sales industry that used the term *objection* to describe this. No one is objecting to anything; however, we all have concerns. We are concerned about spending too much for a product or service, we are concerned about whether someone will perform as promised, and we are concerned about making the best decision among the options available to us. This is where our communication skills are put to the test.

When someone voices a concern, I recommend you avoid responding immediately. Instead, everyone is better served when you repeat the concern aloud, assuring you understand it accurately. You may say something like this: "So to make sure I am interpreting you correctly . . ." Then repeat what the person stated. You accomplish some important things by doing so. First, you have made an assertive effort to assure that you understand the person's position; thus, you are likely to avoid responding inappropriately. Second, the other party knows you are paying attention and showing respect. Once you have a clear understanding of another's position, it is appropriate to isolate the concern. Ask if anything else is preventing the person from moving forward. If so, listen closely and repeat the process we have just reviewed until everything is on the table. Then begin addressing concerns one by one.

When people's concerns appear to be without merit, or they just cannot seem to offer a sound explanation as to why they have taken a particular position on something, it can be a sign that money is the real issue. When your proposal involves a financial commitment, odds are the concerns have a great deal to do with the money required to move forward. When money is not the obstacle, it is likely the perceived value of what they will receive in exchange for their money is. You have undoubtedly failed to this point to establish the value of your product, service, or idea. This is not necessarily a problem; you may still seal the deal, but only when you know exactly what the other person is thinking.

Many people hate to reveal their financial condition and will present you with countless excuses to avoid the possibility of it even becoming a topic of discussion. Whether money is the issue or an unanswered question is the issue, you need to find out while you are still present with them. Should you part company before knowing what is preventing them from moving forward, your proposal will seldom receive the consideration it deserves.

Should a prospective client state that money is indeed the issue, you will want to isolate what exactly it is about the money that presents a problem. Ask, "Were money of no concern, would there be any additional obstacles to moving forward at the present time?" Always make sure you have isolated the concern prior to addressing it. My assumption here is that you have isolated and addressed everything to this point, and we are truly focused on the one remaining obstacle — appropriating the funds to facilitate the order. Asking what aspect of the money presents the problem provides you an opportunity to gain insight into what is really going on in the prospect's mind. You want to find out how you can help the prospect overcome the obstacle. Together you can investigate possibilities the person might not have considered. People are generally grateful for assistance and persistence. Just make sure you have correctly identified their wants and needs, and that you are working to put them first.

Obviously, money may not be the issue. The real issue may be caution. Good for them! I can appreciate the wisdom in taking caution, but I can also appreciate the urgency with which some opportunities must be addressed. Let them know you appreciate them for carefully considering their decisions and that you are thankful for the opportunity to provide them with all of the pertinent information required to make an educated decision. Then ask them what questions they still have. Remember to isolate the questions. Make sure each response you provide meets their satisfaction before moving forward to address their next question. Once you have covered all of their questions, offer some incentive for them to move forward immediately—if necessary. Otherwise, ask them when they will likely make a decision. Then ask permission to follow up, and keep your commitment. Remember, persistence pays dividends.

The Importance of Honesty

When you adhere to the five steps of influence as outlined, you will find the sale is usually made during the discovery and recommendation process. An honest exchange during discovery and recommendation promotes a cooperative alliance between the parties. Remember, the nurturing of healthy, constructive relationships is critical to achieving success. From time to time you may encounter individuals who choose not to participate in an honest exchange. When this happens, you will be better off walking away despite what you think you may lose.

People who have trouble being real, choosing instead to remain guarded, are not worth the aggravation they cause. Fortunately, most people are sincere the majority of the time. Relationships typically flourish when approached with sincerity. When we are unwilling to settle for less than honesty, we will be recognized and embraced by those who seek the same in return. When there has been an honest exchange in the discovery and recommendation between parties, a natural agreement should have already been reached. There are only four reasons the parties will fail to come to an agreement: (1) someone has failed to be honest. (2) Someone is creating an emotional block, preventing progress between the parties. (3) Not everyone recognizes the value in proceeding. (4) Financial issues remain.

Good or bad, emotions are frequently a driving force behind decisions. Our emotions play a critical role in determining the outcome of our lives. The feelings we have may cloud our ability to think things through and can result in poor decision making. Our emotions can also be a tremendous ally in helping us achieve success. As we are moved by our emotions to take action, so too can we move others through their emotions. Ultimately, the stronger emotions prevail.

Many people make the majority of their decisions based on how they feel and then justify their actions, seeking information to support their rationale. Our emotions are a marvelous medium we can use to catapult to new levels of success by motivating ourselves as well as others into action.

The following example may provide some insight as to how you can harness the emotions of others, and thus motivate them to do what is in their best interest:

While employed by a Fortune 50 company, I called on a prospective account. I had barely entered the premises when I was greeted by an exceptionally hostile man. This man, whom I will call Mr. Roberts, called me every name imaginable with the exception of my own. I froze in my tracks, remaining silent as he continued to colorfully articulate his displeasure with the company I represented. Mr. Roberts believed he had been wronged, and he simply desired to vent. Having determined I was not in any danger, I stood my ground and listened to what he had to say, cautious not to interrupt him. Only when he finished did I dare speak. I knew not to attempt to defend the company—this would only further incite his rage. It would be in my best interest to distance myself from the company as quickly as possible. This man had to see me as an individual, not some corporate minion. I told him I was at a disadvantage, not being certain what had led to his indignation. In my attempt to reduce the tension, I joked that I had no recollection of ever having dated his daughter. I caught him off guard with this remark, and to my good fortune it was effective; he actually chuckled. I told him I was sincerely concerned about what had transpired, and I asked what I might do to rectify the situation. He was more than happy to fill me in.

Apparently, this man owned and operated a number of retail stores, some of which were located more than 2,500 miles away, on the East Coast of the United States. He purchased advertising for these locations a few years prior from the company I was representing. He explained that my company had launched its new Florida directory after losing the contract with the phone company with which it was now competing. What had left him disgruntled was though the directory I represented initially undercut the pricing of the primary directory by more than forty percent, within three years we were charging as much as the competition. This transpired even though my company only controlled a minority share of the market. Roberts said his advertising costs, as a result, had doubled in order for his business to maintain the original presence previously provided by one directory. Though he appreciated the benefits competition traditionally afforded the consumer, a new directory was the last thing he desired to see introduced to the local market. When he had previously been down this road, it cost him an additional $30,000 a year. I now understood why he was so upset.

I made sure not to interrupt Roberts while he filled me in, waiting for the right opportunity to offer my assessment of the situation. Once he had his say, he calmed right down. Now I could respond.

"Mr. Roberts, if I were in your shoes, I would be just as upset as are. Unfortunately, the directory now has a presence in this market as well—another victory for the ever-expanding free enterprise system," I said sarcastically. I went on to tell him there was little question as to whether the new directory would successfully capture a respectable percentage of the existing market share and thus his potential customers.

He mumbled something resembling "yeah," followed by an expletive. I then asked him what percentage of his sales could be attributed to the directory each year for the past three years, and what dollar volume this represented to his bottom line. It turned out to be a substantial amount—so substantial that his business would suffer as the new directory's market share expanded, penetrating the monopoly the primary directory had sustained for so long. I then told him it was not a question as to whether he should have a presence in the new directory, but rather how large his presence should be in order to ensure his business would continue to capture its share of the market. As any astute business professional would, he placed his emotions aside, opting to perform in accordance with the best interests of his company. It was the second year the directory had been published and distributed in this market, but it would be Mr. Roberts' first local advertisement with us.

Mr. Roberts revealed himself at the onset of our introduction. His emotions indicated his attachment to a specific outcome. He understood his business would incur losses if he failed to advertise with the new directory, and it irritated him. His expenditure would double only to retain the exposure his business had previously received with the one directory. All I had to do was listen to what he had to say. As he shared with me his frustrations, I learned all I needed to know. I was then in a position to serve him, and by appealing to his rationale, Mr. Roberts placed his emotions aside in order to objectively approach what was clearly an economic decision. It is true — understanding and patience pays dividends.

Roberts could easily have remained belligerent, choosing not to transact business with the company he considered responsible for his dilemma. In his attempt to even the score, his business would have suffered, offering him little solace in exchange for retribution. I was happy to play a role in preventing this. After all, Mr. Roberts was not a bad man. I was prepared, regardless of how unique the circumstances were, to handle Roberts' demeanor because I had learned a systematic approach in moving beyond superficial exchange.

People who approach their lives and businesses systematically get what they want. They leave as little as possible to chance. They are usually the same individuals who fall into opportunity with relative ease and do so with consistency. Success happens when preparedness meets opportunity. Systems also reduce the likelihood of us overlooking something critical with respect to our performance. A system often consists of little more than the implementation of a well-thought-out checklist of things to do that was previously proven effective. I have frequently recommended Michael Gerber's *E-Myth Revisited* to my coaching clients. This book offers significant insight into the power provided to businesses and personal lives when we choose to systemize our activities. Systems streamline our efforts, eliminate duplication, increase productivity, reduce errors, and help minimize aggravations.

You will become more effective and more prosperous when mapping your course prior to submersing yourself in your endeavors; it is much easier to hit a target you see clearly. As I have previously stated, you do not have to possess the answers at the onset; in fact, it is unlikely you will. Do not make the mistake of remaining idle because you are uncertain as to the best course of action. Seek assistance and you will find it. Begin planning based on the information you have, and adjust your itinerary as needed. Once having charted your course, you will want to periodically reevaluate your performance. You will likely have to make adjustments from time to time, most everyone does. Constantly remind yourself of your purpose, and rest assured with determination and persistence, you will find what you seek.

I will make one final point with respect to my encounter with Mr. Roberts. I was fairly confident in my ability to earn his business from the onset because I have come to understand that anger is often a byproduct of one's emotional attachment to a specific outcome. Had Mr. Roberts not cared, he would have likely been indifferent rather than angry, and he certainly would not have given me the time of day.

What is the opposite of love? Here's a clue; it isn't hate. Both love and hate typically require us to retain some form of attachment to the party we project our feelings towards. Both love and hate are driven by emotion. When you hate someone, that person still has some level of influence over you. Chances are your hatred carries a cost far greater to you than to the person you hate. Your anger has absolutely no effect on the other person; yet you continue to waste good energy and, in the process, attract negative energy. Lousy situation, isn't it? There is nothing to gain and everything to lose when we choose to waste precious energy hating someone. We are far better off projecting good will toward the person, thus attracting energy that will enrich rather than deplete our vitality.

The true opposite of love is indifference. When we are indifferent, we are void of any emotional attachment to a specific individual or outcome. Neither the individual nor the outcome to which we are indifferent has any perceived influence in our lives — unless the person is someone we cannot avoid. Retaining hatred for another may indicate we are remaining attached with respect to the way the person makes us feel about ourselves. The fact is, when we blame others for the suffering endured by hating them, we grant them power over us.

In closing this session, I emphasize how valuable the five steps of influence will be in creating the life you desire. This formula is the best there is for opening the pathway to opportunity. Remember, highly successful people are typically adept at communicating what they want and just as proficient in uncovering the needs and desires of others.

Session 11 Summary

The Five Steps of Influence:

1. Introduction
2. Discovery
3. Recommendation
4. Call to Action
5. Isolate and Address Concerns

- An honest exchange is vital to your successful communication.
- Decisions are frequently based on emotions and then justified.
- Systems simplify the process and maximize the outcome.

Your Exercises for the Week

1. Review your master things-to-do list. Select a task requiring the assistance of another, and act on it.
2. Create your introduction and outline the discovery you will use to *sell* your proposal.
3. Conducting yourself in accordance with the five-step formula, meet with an individual and determine if his needs and desires are aligned with the solutions you are offering.
4. Note the results from your exchange, and analyze how your discovery could have been more effective in preparing for concerns the person may have expressed.

5. Adjust your recommendations to preempt the concerns identified in your discovery.

Session Review

SESSION 12
RISE TO LIFE'S ULTIMATE CHALLENGE!

Welcome to Session 12 and the completion of this series with your personal coach. The ultimate challenge we face is putting into practice what we have learned. In many instances, this requires a great deal of repetition—hence, my asking you to review each session as we progressed. Doing so may have at first appeared redundant; yet, you have undoubtedly discovered something about yourself along the way.

I hope you have found yourself inspired, increasingly optimistic, and more determined as a result of these sessions. Considering everyone faces some form of negativity daily at work, at home, in the car, and on the news, we must make a concerted effort to seek out the positive. Your results likely will not improve much should you choose to act on the principles only sporadically. You must make them a daily ritual in your life; they must become a habitual extension of who you are. Remember the words of Aristotle: "Excellence is not an act, but a habit."

Every day we make decisions, all of which alter our life in the days, weeks, months, and years to come. Some may decide change requires more effort than they are willing to put forth and therefore remain stagnant. I hope you have decided to become a better person with the arrival of each day. We all share one inescapable reality: we cannot change the number of hours in a day. Instead, what we choose to do with those hours makes all the difference.

We all have a choice. We posses the discretion to do with our lives as we wish, to make the most of the time we have, or to waste it doing nothing constructive—this is not to say we do not require or deserve rest and relaxation (just avoid unwinding so much so that you lose the spring in your step). There is no denying the actions we take today will reflect in the results of our tomorrow. So, for those of you unwilling to settle for anything less than the magnificence for which you were created, do something about it here and now!

For those of you who picked up this book and used it as it was intended, twelve weeks have passed from the time you were first asked to closely examine the current state of your life. Provided you have complied with my requests, completing the exercises at the close of each session, you have gained new critical insights into who you really are and what you truly desire. Additionally, you have been reminded of, or for the first time exposed to, the principles that will assist you in creating whatever you desire to become, acquire, or accomplish. You should be well on your way to achieving excellence in managing your life as never before. This is the first and consequently, a critical step in attaining your dreams.

In this session, we will review the highlights of the previous eleven sessions, pulling them together to create a comprehensive instructional guide or master list of things to do. You will want to keep this in a place that will allow you easy access to it daily.

✓ **What Matters Most?**

The purpose of Session 1 was for you to determine what you want out of your life—to choose your destination. You should by now find yourself reassessing your priorities, if you have not done so already. I assume you have determined what you would like to do with your life. I also hope you have decided to quit procrastinating and to *just do it!* You may not have much time—unfortunately none of us knows just how much time we have. Live with the urgency of one who has been informed they are dying. This should give you a completely different perspective in life, helping you to assess what is most important. Do something remarkable—something worth having lived for.

✓ **Expect a Miracle**

There are times we could all use a miracle. We need the faith miracles inspire as much as the results they provide. The problem with many of us is we simply do not expect miracles; thus we do not experience them as often as we otherwise would. When you choose to ask for a miracle, discard your doubt and negativity, and the universe will go to work on your behalf. Remember to avoid people or situations draining you of your vital energy and distracting you from your focus. Keep the faith. Good comes from life's tribulations.

Forgive those who have slighted you. Accept the perfection of your design, and aspire to achieve your full potential. You can accomplish far more than you have likely believed possible. Challenge your perceptions every day. It is your responsibility to do everything within your power to be the best you can be. You alone must determine who and what you will become.

✓ Know Thyself

This session provided a gateway for you to recognize who you are at the core level. You should have created a Personal Identity Declaration to assist you in planning and prioritizing your life's ambitions. This will also serve you in living harmoniously with your true values. You have learned you have far more control over your thoughts than you may have once believed. A simple decision is all that is required to alter the course of your life. Make it a habit to use positive words and phrases that will empower you: "I'll do it," not "I'll try." Be assured all people face adversity. Champions possess the determination to rise above hardship, allowing nothing and no one to hold them back from their dreams. What would you accomplish were you unstoppable? You *are* unstoppable; you must only believe! Everything begins with how you are thinking and what you choose to focus on.

✓ Imitate the Masters

All of us know people we admire for their accomplishments in sports, the arts, business, and so forth. These individuals have something in common, originating in their attitude. They feel deserving of the success they have attained. They have a healthy perspective about life, humanity, and their own self-worth. They recognize the gifts they posses and do not hesitate to utilize them.

To accomplish your own objectives in life, emulate the attitudes and behavior of those who have accomplished the very things you desire to achieve. Seek out these individuals, study their biographies, read their publications, and associate with them. I do not recommend you strive to be their clone. Maintain your individuality while adopting the favorable characteristics of those who have paved the trail before you. There is so much negativity in the world around us. We must be careful to seek out positive people and environments conducive to fostering our success.

✓ **Commit Yourself**

The force of gravity increases as the mass of a body or planet increases. Size determines gravitational force. In like manner, the size of our commitment will determine the extent to which we attract the success we desire. Once again, I will draw upon the words of Napoleon Hill: "The simple act of commitment is a powerful magnet for help." Use "I am" statements to ignite the law of attraction, and draw upon the power of this magnificent force to support your endeavors. Ask questions of yourself and others that promote solutions rather than prolong problems. Look to the possibilities to which you aspire. Commit and recommit every day, remain focused on your objective, be patient, and have faith that the solutions you seek will be revealed.

Most significant discoveries, accomplishments, and human undertakings did not result from the efforts of those who possessed answers and knowledge prior to undertaking their challenge.

Though they likely had a clear vision of the outcome they desired, they typically possessed little insight as to how they might accomplish their goal. They are the ones who bravely marched into the unknown, confident their inquisitive nature would reveal the world's riches. It takes courage to be different, strength to persist, and faith to unveil the mysteries of life. *Commit yourself, and the road will be paved before you.*

✓ **Prioritize**

You have your list of things to do. Which thing among them is the most important to you? Few of us can do multiple tasks well at the same time. Delegate whenever possible. Preserve your energy to complete the tasks you have identified as most important. Time and energy are finite; utilize them on the high-priority tasks first, and then move to those you have identified as less important. Prioritize daily to assure you accomplish what is truly important. You will typically find your rewards in proportion to your efforts.

Many people take the path of least resistance and end up at the bottom of the hill. Those who prioritize choose an upward path and end up at the top of the mountain. The resistance you experience in you upward climb should be associated with progress. Anything significant is seldom accomplished without experiencing resistance — resistance is frequently an indicator that you are on the right path. View resistance positively, remembering if it were easy, everyone would be doing it.

✓ **Plan to Succeed**

Virtually everything—your home, car, anything you may own or use—was manufactured by someone using a plan, schematic, or architectural design. Isn't it interesting how we haphazardly approach our lives? We act as though we will accomplish something significant flying by the seat of our pants, while the simplest of items requiring assembly often cause us to utter the phrase, "When all else fails, read the instructions." Part of the price we must pay for success is time and energy invested in a plan. Skip the plan, and you will find yourself spending far more time and energy to accomplish far less.

At this point, take your list of things to do and break it down into small steps—from where you are to where you want to be. Begin with the resources available to you. As you move through the steps in your plan, you will find yourself adjusting to make use of new insights and resources introduced to you while moving closer to achieving your objective.

Action is little more than a descriptive term for movement. When you are moving, you are experiencing an ever-changing environment that will alter your perspective. Be flexible—a new perspective will promote the introduction of new possibilities. Whatever your desire, you will accomplish it faster and with less effort by mapping your course in advance. Remember, most people do not plan to fail, they fail to plan; thus they fail.

✓ **Take Massive and Immediate Action**

Many of you have accomplished more in recent weeks than some accomplish in their lifetime. You have a greater understanding of who you are and what you value most in life. The fact you have completed this book indicates that you not only possess the desire to progress, you also possess the commitment to do so. Congratulations! Your greatest ambitions will be fulfilled, building on the principles you have learned, as long as you continue to press forward. *There is no benefit in acquiring knowledge when you fail to act on it.*

Everything you have done to this point places you at the trailhead which will lead to the top of your personal mountain. You are now equipped with all you need to begin your ascent. Any additional knowledge, skill, or introduction you may need to reach your destination will present itself along the way.

✓ **Opportunities Abound**

Opportunities are everywhere, and success happens when preparedness meets opportunity. We must learn to see what others fail to see. By learning and applying life's critical lessons, you are preparing yourself to recognize and embrace surrounding opportunities. You are now likely more attuned with the principle of attraction. As a result, you will find yourself attracting more of what you truly desire. Be open. What appears to be impossible for some will be possible at some point and time for another. Always remember, action illuminates opportunity.

✓ **Serve Others Well**

Service takes many forms. Serve others as they wish to be served. You simply cannot serve without finding someone serving you in turn. You cannot out-give a giver. Give away the very things you desire and they will return to you many fold. Practice serving without expectation, and begin receiving by first learning to pay it forward!

✓ **The Five Steps of Effective Influence**

Most anything you aspire to accomplish will require the assistance of others. You will be far more likely to receive the assistance you seek when you follow the steps outlined. Review this session as often as needed to become comfortable with the sequence and then follow it. With practice, you will achieve great results. Discovery is a powerful tool that will provide you the insight necessary to present authoritative recommendations in accordance with the needs and desires of those you seek to serve. Success is fleeting when we fail to place the interests of others above our own. Understanding the attitudes and mindsets of others will assist you in making recommendations that will benefit all parties. Approach everyone with the goal of understanding and serving them, and you will prosper.

The Five Steps of Influence are designed to promote understanding, honesty, and trust. The systematic format of the process virtually assures you will consistently experience a positive exchange when presenting your ideas, products, or services.

Congratulations!

You made it. I commend you for investing the time, energy, and thought required to complete these twelve sessions with your personal coach. I know this has been difficult for some of you, and I am sure it has been challenging for most. Those of you who have adhered to my recommendations, approaching the material within these pages with a sincere desire to improve, have gained insights, skill sets, and a heightened perspective with respect to your potential. To those of you who read but did not participate in the exercises, I ask you to reconsider completing the exercises. You will gain much by doing so!

I have coached many people from all walks of life who have prospered because they chose to follow the advice within the pages of this book. Their prosperity had little to do with where they came from or what they may have at one time perceived to be true. They came to know themselves and others better than they had before. They learned to approach life as though nothing were impossible for them to achieve. They learned to have faith and to define themselves and their life's purpose. They came to understand that they were not alone. It is empowering to reach this understanding. It is even more empowering when you choose to approach everything in life in accordance with this truth. Provided you have followed my recommendations, you now know yourself as you never did before. You possess a clearly defined Personal Identity Declaration, a prioritized list of things to do, and at minimum, a roughly drafted plan on how you intend to accomplish your objectives. With all this being completed, you only require the faith that what you ask for will be granted, the wisdom to ask, and the courage to do your part.

Of all my objectives in writing this book, the most important is my desire to convey to you just how remarkable you are. Your genetics, your experiences, your imagination, and your attitude combined, distinguish you from any other. You exist to think, create, love, and nurture all that is good. It is time for you to achieve what others may believe is impossible. It is time you embrace your greatness and the perfection of your design. Go now and let your works illuminate the world.

Be blessed!

A CLOSING LETTER

Dear Friend:

When I began writing *Your Personal Coach: Achieving Excellence in Life* in November 2004, I had no idea as to the severity of the resistance my family and I would experience. Our faith was put to the test. I shared with my wife my desire to write a book that would positively affect the lives of many. I had talked of writing such a book for close to three years, and I was haunted by the fact that I had put it off for so long. The timing, she pointed out, could not have been worse.

The previous year I had diverted my attention, time, and financial resources to the management of a medical company, in which I owned an interest. Originally, I was to serve merely in an advisory capacity; however, I soon found myself immersed in the daily operations of the business. I believe in miracles, and I imagine this is why I never hesitated to write this book at such an inconvenient time. To me it was unreasonable and therefore the best course of action. I told my wife, "Have faith. God will provide." And he did.

Not long after I began writing, the medical company began making money — not a great deal but it was certainly an improvement. This was good news, though little compensation for the adversity we were about to face. During the next four months (the time required for me to write the first draft), our home flooded; my daughter, her good friend, and I were involved in an auto accident, totaling my car; and not long after that, we had a kitchen fire. This, as it is said, was only the tip of the iceberg. I also came to discover the individual I had entrusted with the financial management of the medical company had been embezzling since the beginning. It is one thing to suffer financially, it is quite another to endure the loss of a friendship. I have never experienced such a concentrated chain of negative events in such a brief period of time.

Now it gets even more interesting. Once I completed my draft, the adversity subsided. Life then took a new direction. I was reunited with my father's sister and her children—the ones I spoke of in the first chapter. We had lost contact twenty-three years prior. Their searching paid off and they found me. I also had the good fortune to meet family for the first time. Family I had not previously known existed. As if being reunited with my family was not blessing enough, my aunt informed me in the following weeks that I was to receive an inheritance—enough to offset the financial loss I had incurred while dedicating my time to writing this book. Mark this up to coincidence if you will, but as you know by now, I do not believe in coincidence. I share this with you only so you may know I truly believe God does in fact work in mysterious ways. I admit, however, I do not find his ways so mysterious any longer; rather, I expect miracles, both big and small.

I completed the draft in the spring of 2005 and published a limited number of copies that made their way into circulation. Still, I knew there was more I needed to share—subject matter that cried out to be addressed with greater clarity. Recognizing this, I placed the project on hold, pulled the book from the presses and stepped back from the project long enough to thoroughly review my work. I am grateful I chose to do so, regardless of the challenge. In the end I have the satisfaction of completing a difficult task that demanded my best.

The opportunity to serve you has been my privilege. Thank you for permitting me to fulfill my dream of sharing with you the principles that have provided me an abundance of life's precious gifts. I wish you success in achieving your own dreams. May all that is good be yours this day and throughout your life. Live in faith, be bold, look to the unreasonable, and understand all the good you seek has always been and always will be yours for the asking.

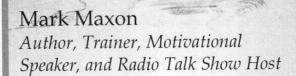

Mark Maxon
Author, Trainer, Motivational Speaker, and Radio Talk Show Host

Now three decades into his career, Mark has been trained and employed by both Fortune 500 and Fortune 50 companies. In August of 1997, Mark founded Lifeworks International, a Life and Business development organization dedicated to assisting others in achieving their dreams. Over the course of the last decade, Mark has coached hundreds of aspiring individuals to attain heightened levels of success in multiple areas of their lives.

Known for his demand for excellence and daring vision, Mark is recognized as one of the most captivating speakers in the motivational and sales training industry. Now, he will inspire you to do what is necessary to truly live the life you desire. Mark is refreshingly genuine in his delivery; he possesses the hands-on experience his audience and readers can relate to. Most importantly, within these pages, Mark offers the reader a systematic process for creating personal success that works. For those seeking a realistic approach to improving their life, this book is a must read!

Mark, his wife Tresha, and their youngest son presently reside in South Jordan, Utah. For online access to broadcasts of The Maxon Show, visit **www.themaxonshow.com.**

For contact information and or to request Mark for speaking engagements, business consulting, sales training, or personal coaching, log on to **www.themaxongroup.com**.

Made in the USA
Charleston, SC
17 February 2013